CAMBRIDGE COACH SERVICES

FROM THE DRIVER'S SEAT
BY JIM NEALE

Copyright © Jim Neale 2013   All rights reserved
ISBN 978-0-9575996-0-4
Published by Burbus Publications
'Daimville', 2, Chestnut Rise,
BURWELL, Cambridge CB25 0BX

By the same author:
Burwell & District Motor Service Illustrated History
First published 1978, reprinted 2011 & 2013
My Favourite Coach 932 BCE, first published 2012

Projected Title
My Favourite Bus 9 DER

Designed by Burwell Community Print Centre
www.burwellprint.co.uk

Printed by Colchester Press

CONTENTS

APPENDICES

Cover photo by **Richard Haughey**

FOREWORD

To publish a book about the history of a coach company that was only in existence for ten years may seem unusual but the story of Cambridge Coach Services (CCS) encompasses a much longer period. The story goes from the expansion and demise of Premier Travel (PT), to becoming part of a group of companies that flourished in the wake of de-regulation of the passenger transport industry. There is no doubt that CCS would never have come about without the foresight and determination of one man, Ian Neville Roberts.

His extensive experience in the passenger transport industry helped to influence the latter years of PT after he was appointed Assistant General Manager in 1984 by the founder Edward Arthur Lainson and the Matthews brothers, Frank and John. They had hoped to secure the future of their company, which was established in 1936 and had been a pioneer in express coach operation across the country, usually in co-operation with other operators rather than in competition.

The CCS fleet was mainly comprised of Plaxton-bodied Volvos, with some earlier Van Hool bodies on the same chassis inherited from the PT fleet on the formation of the company. This book is not only about the coaches but also the routes and people that were employed by CCS. Many started as drivers, receiving encouragement from Ian Roberts to progress throughout the company, some achieving successful careers within the coaching industry.

The sudden death of Ian Roberts in May 1997 saw a gradual change of policy from his intentions leading to the sale of the company in 1999. By then it had become desirable to be absorbed into the national network. Ironically some of the coaches that formed the initial fleet were new in National Express (NatEx) livery, albeit owned by PT as a contractor. Most of the vehicles bought new by CCS were subsequently painted in NatEx livery as part of their 'Owned Operations' fleet. This gives scope to illustrate the same coach in more than one livery.

To collect all the relevant information together for this book has taken me some time and I am grateful to former CCS employees for their assistance and encouragement. As I worked for PT for six years prior to the split when Cambus Holdings Ltd (CHL) took part of the company, I had some insight into both sides. I later drove part-time for both CCS and Premier Travel Services (PTS), as CHL had renamed the coaching side of their business. I then returned as a full-time driver with CCS up until the takeover by AirLinks in 1999, becoming a part-time driver for NatEx until they closed the Cambridge depot that had in turn been the Headquarters of both PT and CCS.

Fortunately I still have most of the Staff Bulletins and more than 40 of my own diaries, which have recorded most of the vehicles I have driven since passing my driving test. My collection of old timetables and some loaned by others has enabled me to record so many details. Having failed the eleven plus exam, my literary talents are somewhat limited, so I must thank well known transport authors Geoff Mills, Paul Carter and my sister Marion Standing for their editorial advice, also my daughter-in-law Jenny Neale for help with computer-related matters. Acknowledgement is also due to the records of The Omnibus Society, PSV Circle and Cambridge Omnibus Society, along with the many photographers who have made their work available to me, making the final selection a difficult task.

By its very nature this book will be somewhat unconventional and autobiographical,

I propose to call it:-

CAMBRIDGE COACH SERVICES FROM THE DRIVER'S SEAT

Jim Neale
Burwell
April 2013

AUTHOR'S INTRODUCTION

As I claim to write this book 'from the driver`s seat', it could be appropriate to summarise my previous experience in this position. Starting off as a bus conductor with Burwell & District Motor Services (B&D), I passed my PSV driving test on 4 August 1970, a few days after my twenty-first birthday. Driving a 1962 AEC Renown double-decker with manual gearbox gave me an 'all groups' licence which enabled me to drive any type of PSV in the UK at the time, although I have subsequently been required to undergo 'type training' by prospective employers.

Burwell & District 1970-1979

Eastern Counties June - Sept. 1979

Young`s Coaches 1979-1982

For almost nine years I drove buses and coaches for B&D on a variety of work, including stage carriage, contracts, private hire, excursions and seasonal express services. B&D were taken over by Eastern Counties (EC), the local National Bus Company (NBC) operator in June 1979. The vehicles were not retained but staff were taken on if they wished, as there was no redundancy offered.

I drove for EC for three months from the Burwell depot, which was an outstation of Newmarket, mainly red Bristols on the ex B&D routes, which the Traffic Commissioners insisted were maintained for a time. EC were also obliged to operate the summer express services to Great Yarmouth and Felixstowe, plus any excursions or private hire that B&D had on their books at the time of takeover. Coaching requirements were met by sending a coach from the Cambridge depot, to be driven by a Burwell based driver if one was available. This situation led me to my first drive in a white National coach, giving me brief experience of Leyland Leopards and Bristol RE`s. Little did I then realise how many white liveried coaches I would drive later on in my career.

Most of the former B&D drivers were not happy working for EC and left. I also left after three months, going to work for Young`s Coaches at Rampton, driving Bedford and DAF coaches on a variety of work that included contracts, tours and private hire. Some of these runs were reliefs on hire to National Express (NatEx), mostly entailing driving empty into London and following National coaches from Victoria Coach Station (VCS) to places like Liverpool, Burnley, Sunderland and Newcastle. These journeys always involved an overnight stay and return journey, which was much more ambitious than anything I had done with B&D.

Three years later found me working for Premier Travel (PT), once again driving AEC Reliances that were familiar from B&D days. As my coach was based at home, core duties were Pye works and local school contracts and anything that could be fitted in between. It was not long before I was allocated a Leyland Leopard and regular overnight runs on Birmingham and Rochdale routes, operated jointly with NatEx and Yelloway. There were also occasional trips to Oxford and Lowestoft, not forgetting of course, the airport runs from Cambridge, which would become familiar to me as they were expanded and developed into part of the NatEx network.

There were big changes at PT in 1988, when Cambus Holdings Ltd (CHL) almost succeeded in acquiring PT but were beaten at the last moment by a staff/ management buyout, backed by Yorkshire based AJS Holdings. This will be looked at in a later chapter but the upshot was that many of the original PT drivers became disenchanted with the changes in operation and left for various reasons. I was one of them and after six years with PT, was fortunate to find a job in a factory close to home making wooden pallets and cardboard containers. This suited me at the time, also enabling me to sometimes drive coaches at weekends. After three years in the factory my employers found they could buy in ready-made pallets cheaper than we could make them. As a result they closed the factory and I was made redundant.

At that time I was involved in the development of family land, which enabled me to take on part-time driving with the newly established Cambridge Coach Services (CCS) and CHL-owned Premier Travel Services (PTS), as well as an occasional shift on the Guide Friday Cambridge City Tour. Some weeks I found myself working more hours in total than I would if I was full-time with just one employer, which led me to become a full-time driver for CCS on 30 May 1994.

In October 1999 CCS was sold to AirLinks, at that time part of the NatEx group. Once again, the transitional period proved interesting, and will be covered in more detail later on. The driving rotas were not to my liking, leading me to apply for one of the newly created jobs of cleaner/shunter based at Kilmaine Close in Cambridge. I worked 12 hour night shifts, four on/four off from May 2000 until September 2001, when I was able to return to part-time employment. This included frequent driving shifts of what had by then become Jetlink vehicles, which in turn were painted into white NatEx livery. These included the former CCS coaches until the Cambridge depot was closed in February 2005.

Premier Travel 1983-1988

I tried the option of transferring to the Start Hill depot, near Stansted Airport, where former Cambridge operations were based for a month, but decided instead to drive still part-time for Burtons Coaches. They were then run by Paul Cooper and had contracted to operate the 010 and 787 services with new coaches in NatEx livery based at the Stagecoach depot at Newmarket, closer to my home. This worked well for me, until in October 2005 Burtons decided to transfer their NatEx operations to their main depot at Haverhill, 26 miles away. I continued with Burtons, driving services 787 Cambridge – Heathrow, 727 Stansted – Norwich and the Friday and Sunday service 314 Cambridge – Birmingham. This was a route familiar to me from my days with PT and the service 70 operated briefly by CCS in 1994.

Burtons lost the 727 and 787 contracts in August 2008 but retained part of the 010 and weekend 314, so I continued to drive the 314 when required. At the same time I renewed my acquaintance with NatEx-owned operations at Start Hill, back on my familiar 787 route from September 2008. For some time Burtons Coaches had been part of the Tellings Golden Miller (TGM) group, who in turn had been taken over by Arriva. Burtons eventually returned to independent ownership under Yellow Star Travel Services. As TGM retained the remaining NatEx contracts, they were allocated to the TGM group Excel Logistics` depot at Stansted Airport from August 2009. At this point I decided that if I had to drive 35 miles each way to work, then I might as well drive exclusively for NatEx at Start Hill, as the wages and conditions were superior.

Cambridge Coach Services 1991-1999

I drove my last service 314 to Birmingham on 28 August 2009 and continued to drive NatEx coaches from Start Hill on a casual basis when required. I enjoyed the opportunity to occasionally drive a coach on express service while I was able, usually between Cambridge and Heathrow. I also co-drove several Sunday journeys from VCS to Sheffield on service 560 and Leeds, service 561 which were double manned. I drove my last NatEx coach from Heathrow to Cambridge via Luton on 18 April 2011. This was appropriate for me, as I had driven this route on and off for around 20 years.

Early in 2011 I suffered from a period of back pain, which precluded me from driving airport coaches for NatEx with the associated heavy luggage handling duties. As my health improved and I was declared 'fit for work' by the DWP, I was approached by Young`s Coaches in June 2012. They had recently restarted operations on a small scale from Haddenham. The welcome resurrection of the familiar name and livery was instigated by the third generation of the family following the death of the founder Ted Young in 2009. Once again I found myself driving DAF and Scania coaches which had previously been used in NatEx service. My coach driving career was moving towards a conclusion, which the looming driver CPC training requirement looked set to terminate a few months short of my natural retirement age, or would it?

National Express 1999-2011

These five coaches (above) were new to Premier Travel Services in May 1988 in National Express livery. Some of them formed part of the initial fleet of Cambridge Coach Services only two years later, along with the others shown (below) in standard Premier colours. This livery was adopted by CCS on its formation, although the silver was soon replaced by grey. **(Both Author)**

Between 1994 and 1999 Cambridge Coach Services purchased 20 new Plaxton Premiere 350-bodied Volvos, all of which eventually carried some form of National Express livery as seen on T325 APP (below). **(Author)**

Chapter 1   PREMIER FINALE

Some might say that Premier Travel (PT) was the oak tree from which the acorn fell and grew to become Cambridge Coach Services (CCS). The history of PT has been well documented in other publications but a brief review of its coaching operations sets the scene for the story of CCS.

Started in 1936 and run on a shoestring, expansion followed through the fifties, sixties and seventies to become an empire which included many Travel Agents across East Anglia. There was also a mixed fleet of buses and coaches engaged on stage carriage, school and works` contracts and an extensive express coach network, along with limited private hire, the latter usually operated by the newer coaches and senior drivers.

The 1980s saw more ambitious expansion into coaching, firstly the acquisition of Percival`s Anglia Coaches, which added some contracts and private hire early in 1983. This coincided with my joining PT as a driver. The coaches were soon replaced in theory by retaining the last six Alexander-bodied Reliances, which had been due for replacement by new Y-reg Leyland Tigers. More important were the premises at Kings Hedges Road in Cambridge which comprised a two-bay workshop, outbuildings and a couple of houses, which were soon converted into offices and drivers` accommodation.

PT was by then in the 'big company' league, having become joint operators with the likes of National Express (NatEx) and Yelloway on express services, there were big plans for expansion. The former Percival`s premises had previously been part of Chivers Farms orchards, the famous Histon-based jam makers. When the Cambridge northern bypass (A45, later to become the A14) was built in the late seventies, dividing Chivers` land, it was separated and sold to Percival`s, who vacated their cramped depot in King Street naming their new depot Arbury Farm Garage.

By the mid-1970s PT had consolidated their operations to a purpose-built depot in Kilmaine Close, Cambridge and although the ex Burgoin depot in Haverhill was retained, most maintenance work was done in Cambridge. The new facilities were extensive but cramped, which only allowed limited parking. Many coaches were still out-stationed with their regular drivers but with the change in style of operations, the former Percival's premises enabled ambitious plans to be made.

A huge investment in an automated bus wash, with dual fuel pumps and extensive hard standing formed phase one of what had been named 'Premier Park' by the winner of a competition amongst staff. Phase two involved the uprooting of the remaining trees from Chivers` orchards and further concrete hard standing, complemented by extensive security fencing and floodlighting of the entire site. In line with the expansion plans, former National Bus Company (NBC) staff had been recruited to assist in running the bus and coach interests. David Hurry came from Eastern Counties (EC) in 1982 as Traffic Manager, followed by Ian Roberts in 1984, who had extensive traffic office experience in places such as Oxford, Cheltenham and Newcastle. Ian`s appointment as Assistant General Manager under John Matthews was to prove significant in the future of the company.

The advertisement that brought Ian Roberts to Cambridge.

Ian Roberts poses with Premier Park staff John Graves and Bernie Gillett at the retirement presentation of driver Cyril Sadler (right) who served Premier Travel in its various forms from 1960 to 1988. **(Author)**

The expansion of tour work led to upgrading of the coach fleet to include some Hi-line coaches, equipped with toilets and coffee machines, facilities not seen before on PT coaches. This started in May 1983 with three Leyland Tigers with Plaxton Paramount 3500 49 seat bodies. They were used initially on Continental Tours for third parties, but in reality spent a lot of time on other work, including contracts, express services and stage carriage, for which they were rather over specified. Two similar vehicles followed, the first in October 1983 being the one thousandth Leyland Tiger chassis produced, which lead to a big publicity launch at Kilmaine Close, followed by entry to the Nice and Brighton coach rallies the following spring.

The one thousandth Leyland Tiger, A638 OEG freshly washed at Cowley Road with similar GFL 527Y, the only Hi-line coach that the author drove on his regular express service from Clacton to Birmingham in February 1984. **(Author)**

A few months later a change of allegiance, reinforcing the patriotic PT policy of buying British involved the introduction of the first MCW Metroliner Hi-liner coach to be supplied to an independent operator. Fictiously registered B1995 PT on the MCW stand at the NEC Motor Show, it subsequently entered service as B192 JVA in December 1984. A further three Metroliners followed in 1985 as B244-6 JVA to a slightly less lavish finish with demountable toilets, enabling 53 seats to be fitted when required. These were early examples and at the time PT had plans to become agents for MCW, offering service facilities in new workshops at Premier Park, due for completion in 1988.

The fourth Premier Metroliner B246 JVA ready to depart from Premier Park on National joint service 879 at 1400 to Rochdale in late 1985. The 'LEICESTER' and 'ROCHDALE' stickers had been supplied by Yelloway staff to driver Geoff Sparrow, a long standing veteran of joint Yelloway routes. **(Author)**

This site would have been part of a complex to provide head office administration facilities for the whole of the Premier Travel Group, which by then had become a major chain of up to 14 travel agencies across East Anglia, with offices in different parts of Cambridge. The cramped site at Kilmaine Close would have been replaced by the new premises at Premier Park, where extensive facilities would have housed the entire fleet, comprising a ten bay state-of-the-art workshop featuring a drive through MOT bay. A separate building incorporating a staff hostel with a canteen and six bedroomed accommodation for drivers brought in from other parts of the country, as there were frequent shortages of steering wheel attendants. In August 1985 a Leyland Royal Tiger Doyen joined the PT touring fleet, for comparison with the Metroliners, which had failed to fulfil expectations, although this British built integral coach did not prove to be much better!

The final expansion happened later in 1985, when the operations of Young's Coaches from nearby Rampton were acquired. As anticipated, much private hire and tours work came with the Young's business, along with several drivers and administration staff. PT hoped to absorb and expand this side of coaching, buying several new and some younger second-hand coaches to replace the former Young's vehicles, most of which were non-standard to the PT fleet. Much new work was generated but there were conflicts of interest between the various types of coaching. Experience has proved that touring and express operations seldom mix successfully, and overlapping of the two can be divisive amongst staff. Most of the former Young's drivers left, other drivers were recruited from a wider area, accommodation was provided for them in company owned houses and thus the new style of operation continued.

Young's vehicles predominate over Premier natives at Premier Park in December 1995. Five Young's DMS Fleetlines joined the five already owned by Premier. They were allocated fleet numbers in the Premier series but retained Young's livery until sale to the new owners of Yelloway for stage carriage use in January 1987. Most of the Young's coaches returned to Rampton for the fleet dispersal auction in February 1986. **(Author)**

Another aspect of the original PT policy of drivers keeping the same coach most of the time was no longer feasible, due to reductions in legal driving time, rest day requirements and the interests of maximum vehicle utilisation. This included the requirement by NatEx to run coaches in their livery on express services. It was decided by management that drivers who operated private hire and express services would have to make their own way to Premier Park to commence duty, sharing coaches in a rostered pool. Those drivers who preferred to continue to keep an allocated coach at home would have an older vehicle, which would be used on the contracts and stage duties usually performed by that driver.

Plaxton-bodied AEC Reliance NEB 349R was allocated to the author in July 1986 when he took an option to keep a coach at home and drive local contracts. He continued to do so until leaving Premier Travel in December 1988. Sometimes referred to as the Burwell outstation of Premier Travel, the farmyard also housed a former Burwell & District preserved bus and coach seen resting in their purpose built sheds. **(Author)**

This operation was masterminded and implemented by Ian Roberts in July 1986 and did not endear him to most of the 'original Premier' drivers, myself included. This meant I would lose the V-reg Leyland Leopard I had driven around 200,000 kilometres over three years. I was allocated an R-reg AEC Reliance for my regular Pye and school contracts, which enabled me to continue to keep a coach at home. Other duties were found for most of us in between our contracts, either on stage carriage, or in the workshops. We became 'contract drivers', after spending most of our time on express services, and in some cases private hire. We were sometimes required to cover express runs when other drivers were not available, usually with the white coach allocated to the journey, although I did several runs to Heathrow in the Reliance.

The Metroliner coaches had not proved as successful as hoped but were kept busy on a variety of work with various drivers. The original enthusiasm and ambition to be a MCW service centre diminished, along with the planned phase three and four developments at Premier Park and the expanded coach operations continued. 'Contract drivers' jogged along in their new roles, some finding satisfaction, others disgruntled and eventually leaving the company.

In another change in vehicle policy, much against the wishes of Mr and Mrs Lainson the first foreign built chassis, a new Volvo B10M but with Plaxton Paramount 3200 body was provided on extended loan in August 1986 and later purchased. This pioneer was followed in 1987 by ten Van Hool-bodied coaches on the same chassis, one of which was fitted with a wheelchair lift to eventually replace the similarly equipped coaches acquired with the Young's business after a period of overlap. These would prove to be the last vehicles bought by the original company and eight of them would form part of the initial CCS fleet in 1990.

*This coach was the first of many Volvo B10Ms to carry the Premier Travel name. The Ayrshire registration of D524 LCS indicated that this coach was intended to be a demonstrator but its success ensured that it became a permanent member of the Premier Travel fleet. Seen at Premier Park when new in August 1986 before the fleet number 341 had been applied, one of the author's duties at the time. (**Author**)*

Premier Travel Services (PTS) was not in such good shape as the more lucrative Premier Travel Agency although the Premier Travel Group as a whole was very profitable. With retirement in mind the board of directors decided to explore the possibilities of selling up. Badgerline Holdings were then a recent product of NBC management buyout and showed an interest. They also owned National Travelworld agencies, which put them in a good position to purchase the whole Premier Travel Group. Prompted by the concerns of management on both sides of the group, the directors decided to separate the two, with the relevant directors retaining the Agency. They then planned to sell PTS to Cambus Holdings Ltd (CHL), which had evolved from the privatisation of part of EC, who made a verbal agreement to buy the company for £1.5 million.

This announcement on 1 December 1987 caused consternation and uproar amongst staff, some middle management probably realising they might not be needed by the new owners. There was also a spirit of independence amongst many others, leading to an alternative bid being formulated by a team of employees led by Ian Roberts. Financial backing came from AJS Holdings, a group based in Yorkshire that had been involved in management buyouts from other NBC companies in that county, the directors of which were already known to Ian Roberts.

The CHL bid was eventually matched by the new consortium, which was seen by the sellers as in the best interests of both staff and passengers, emphasising the long held philosophy of PT management that 'it's all about people'. The management of CHL were understandably aggrieved to be 'pipped at the post' after being led to believe they had a deal, causing subsequent friction between the two companies in the form of competition on local stage carriage services.

At this stage, we find ourselves in a situation with the new PTS, owned by AJS Holdings, run by Ian Roberts as Managing Director, David Hurry as Traffic Manager, Bill Burnett as Company Secretary and Roy Moore as Chief Engineer, with Mick Northfield and Tony Hall as drivers' representatives. The new company ran for a time in conjunction with others in the AJS Group but these were turbulent times in the passenger transport industry. Buying and selling of companies seemed like a game of chance on the monopoly game board to many of us at steering wheel level. Most decisions were made purely on a cost basis, unlike the way the traditional PT company had evolved. The expected date of the takeover by CHL had been 1 January 1988 but the counter bid and subsequent negotiations meant that although the new partnership were expected to take control on the 10 February the final papers were not signed until 0315 on 30 June 1988, after prolonged negotiations!

Ten more Volvo coaches, which had been ordered before the takeover arrived in the Spring of 1988 with Plaxton Paramount 3200 bodies, five were in NatEx livery, the other five in silver/blue. I recall collecting these from Plaxton`s works, travelling up to Scarborough in a West Yorkshire Leyland Leopard which had been on loan to PTS on 20 April with Roy Moore, Ted Young, who provided his trade plates and two other drivers. Plaxtons had removed the Premier Travel Group logos from 363-7, as it was uncertain at one point if they would be diverted elsewhere within the AJS Empire. East Yorkshire Motor Services were mentioned but we drove them back to Cambridge, recording the distance of 322km on the tachograph of E363 NEG. Initially the five coaches ran without fleet names but eventually the new 'PREMIER' logos were applied and they were used mainly on airport routes, replacing the unpopular Metroliners. These would be the last to carry silver paintwork, as it did not wear well and was difficult to match after repair, as can be seen in the picture of D345 KVE on page 18.

The King`s College Chapel outline is synonymous with Cambridge and is shown here incorporated with Premier Travel 'wings' on a 1957 timetable. This design also appeared on uniform caps of the period. The double arrows were incorporated in a new logo to encompass the whole group in 1973.

Ian Roberts re-introduced the College Chapel image on timetables issued in February 1988, retaining the previous typeface briefly until adopting the name 'PREMIER' in Friz Quadrata typeface, a style that would be adopted for 'CAMBRIDGE COACH SERVICES' on its formation.

The new management adopted a grey/blue livery to similar design, with new company logo incorporating an outline of King`s College Chapel. This image had also appeared on some PT timetables as far back as the 1950s. The old style circular double arrow symbol was retained by Premier Travel Agency under their new ownership. The arrival of the five new Volvos in NatEx livery enabled older Leyland Tigers, which also carried that livery, to be repainted into the revised grey/blue livery for general use, or transferred to associated AJS companies.

A factor that has been significant in many company takeovers has been the value of land. Cambridge being a University City, surrounded by hi-tech industry, meant that the value of most bus depots was inflated by the value of the land they occupied. This had been fully exploited by CHL, who had capitalised on several of the former EC depots, re-locating to the outskirts, enabling lucrative re-development of former sites.

This was also relevant to the depots owned by Premier Travel Ltd, which retained ownership of the Head Office at Kilmaine Close and the spacious Premier Park. This site in particular had much commercial potential and had no doubt increased dramatically in value since acquisition from the Moore family with the Percival's coach business. PTS took leases on both Premier Park and the Head Office at Kilmaine Close from the original owners. The former Burgoin premises at Haverhill were also retained by Premier Travel Ltd and soon sold for re-development. PTS were forced to find alternative facilities to refuel and park coaches out-stationed at Haverhill overnight, which were less than ideal.

The high value of commercial land in the Cambridge area continued to affect the viability of the newly established company. Ian Roberts appealed in the August 18 1988 Staff Bulletin for suggestions as to the availability of at least one acre of land close to Cambridge to no avail. At a staff meeting with management on 31 October 1988, Bob Howells, Managing Director of London Country Travel, which at that time was also part of the AJS Group, advised that Premier Park was still owned by Premier Travel Ltd. He also mentioned that the property was valued far too highly to be retained as an operating base, although tenure was secure until March 1990. This gave a breathing space but meant that another site had to be found to secure the long term future of the company, as it was.

With the lease on the depot at Premier Park about to expire, it was no surprise to read in the local press on 24 April 1990 that once again CHL were about to takeover PT. Much to the relief of some staff, it was not to be a total sell-out. Although Managing Director Ian Roberts had been unable to find a suitable site to accommodate the entire PT fleet, he had located premises on an industrial estate at Ely Road, Waterbeach, just off the A10, with space for up to 20 coaches giving good access to Cambridge. These rented premises were not ideal and further from Drummer Street in Cambridge than hoped. At least it was a base from which to form a new company that could continue to operate a sector of the original PT coaches under a new name, thus CCS was born early in May 1990.

The initial CCS fleet comprised eight E-reg Plaxton bodied Volvos and eight D-reg Van Hool-bodied Volvos. Statistics provided by Ian Roberts at the time, claimed that the 16 coaches represented 19% of the PT fleet and would operate 44% of the PT mileage for the new company. This calculation proved to be over optimistic, resulting in the further acquisition of two X-reg Plaxton-bodied Leyland

---

STAFF NOTICE

PREMIER

Post   Remove

NOTICE TO STAFF

You are advised that agreement has been reached for the sale of Premier Travel Services Limited to Cambus Holdings Limited with part of the business being retained by the AJS Group Ltd.

The following work will be sold to Cambus Holdings:-

National Express
Local bus
Plus the majority of works contracts, schools and private hire work.

The AJS Group will retain the following work:-

Company Express 78,79 and 38
Coach Tours
Plus some contract and other coaching activities

The fleet will be split with all vehicles being sold to Cambus Holdings apart from approximately 16 Volvos which will be retained by AJS.

The AJS Group are permitted within the agreement to trade under the name Premier Express for a period of 12 months but will use a different name thereafter.

Premier Travel Services Limited will remain independent of the Cambus bus operating company but an interchange of work is to be expected.

All staff will be advised as to where their future employment lies as soon as possible.

The sale will enable the AJS Group to concentrate on the airport operations in order to gain full benefit from the expansion of Stansted Airport. Those members of staff remaining with Premier will benefit from a rationalisation between Premier and Cambus to improve the overall profitability of coaching activities and promote further expansion.

I will head up the new Company whilst Roy Moore and David Hurry will remain with Premier under its new ownership.

I N Roberts
MANAGING DIRECTOR

Notice No.   Date 23 April 1990   Ref.

The notice posted by Ian Roberts on 23 April 1990 informing staff of their fate as a result of the split in the company. One driver commented that it depended on the part of the wall you sat as to which side you fell! Those who were not happy with their designation were told to find someone else to 'swap' with! **(Brian Sellars)**

Tigers and a solitary T-reg Plaxton-bodied AEC Reliance, all bought new by the original PT. The split of the AJS owned PTS was not straightforward and there was a period of overlap between PT names being removed from the coaches and the new CCS logo being applied. During the transitional period various other PT liveried vehicles could be seen at the Waterbeach depot from time to time. Refuelling was still carried out at Premier Park, until such facilities were installed at Waterbeach by Youngs Engineering, who transferred the diesel tank from Premier Travel's Haverhill depot. There was enough hard standing to park all the coaches and there were also buildings which provided workshop and office accommodation. The proximity of Duffields, the local Volvo Truck and Bus dealer proved to be convenient.

The remainder of the PT fleet passed to CHL, retaining the name 'Premier Travel Services', a name which was to survive into the twenty-first century, as when Cambus sold out to Stagecoach in January 1996 it was carried on several former Premier coaches that had been repainted in corporate stripes livery. Eventually the name was sold to Burtons Coaches from Haverhill, by then run by Paul Cooper who had managed the PTS fleet for CHL until the takeover by Stagecoach. The 'Premier Travel Services' name was used in Burtons publicity and carried on various Burtons liveried coaches, until their sudden demise in May 2011.

A large amount of PTS work at the time of the split was NatEx contracts, which were retained by the new owner. The 14 Plaxton bodied Volvo Expressliners recently acquired on lease joined four similar vehicles already operated by CHL, along with many of the older PTS coaches which had been used on local work. Most of the stage carriage routes were absorbed into the Cambus network.

Plaxton-bodied Volvo E315 OEG illustrates the yellow based Viscount livery that the new Premier Travel Services image was derived from. The author drove this coach for PTS in dual blue half-a-dozen times between 1992-4.
(Ken Worland)

The original Premier Travel Volvo coach D524 LCS shown when new on page ten, seen here at Kilmaine Close in the new PTS livery. The author drove this coach once, on a private hire to Bristol in June 1992.
(Ken Worland)

WEB 408T was one of the last batch of Premier Travel AEC Reliances that gained the simplified version of the new PTS livery. **(Ken Worland)**

The coach fleet was updated, mainly by modern Volvos. A new coach livery based on CHL owned Viscount from Peterborough, with two shades of blue replacing the Viscount yellow/black/grey on the same white base was introduced on Plaxton-bodied Leyland Tiger C332 PEW at an open day held at the Cambus Cowley Road depot on 1 July 1990. This livery soon appeared on most of the PTS front line coaches, with a few remaining AEC Reliances in a simplified version. The Viscount coach fleet gaining 'PREMIER' lettering on their yellow livery until they were eventually repainted into the new CHL Group coach colours. A new depot was opened at Blackstone Road in Huntingdon and coaches were also based at the Viscount depot in Peterborough, resulting in PTS coaches being operated from three different locations.

This brings us to the point where we can now take a closer look at 'CAMBRIDGE COACH SERVICES'

The month of May 1990 saw the emergence of CAMBRIDGE COACH SERVICES (CCS), a new company formed to continue the flagship Airport services developed over the years by Premier Travel (PT). Also included were the daily service 38 from Haverhill to London and 72 seasonal summer service from Haverhill to Bournemouth, both routes had a long history as part of the original PT express network. Other work included as part of the split from Premier Travel Services (PTS), which had become part of Cambus Holdings Ltd (CHL), was a substantial share of Private Hire, Holiday Tours and Excursions, marketed as Classic Day Tours. PTS retained the title of 'Daybreaks' for their excursion programme. This aspect can be seen from the accompanying brochures and press adverts but resulted in both companies competing in the same markets the following year.

The initial ownership of the company appeared to be 'fluid', as at the time AJS Holdings had sold the major part of the group to newly formed Blazefield Holdings. In theory CCS was 'up for sale', which gave rise to many rumours and much speculation that the likes of Badgerline and Speedlink might take over. Blazefield Holdings assumed responsibility for the running but did not own the company at that time. No doubt much to the relief of Ian Roberts and others involved, Blazefield did eventually become the owner. CCS was attached to its Sovereign operations at Stevenage, although several alterations to company names followed over the next few years.

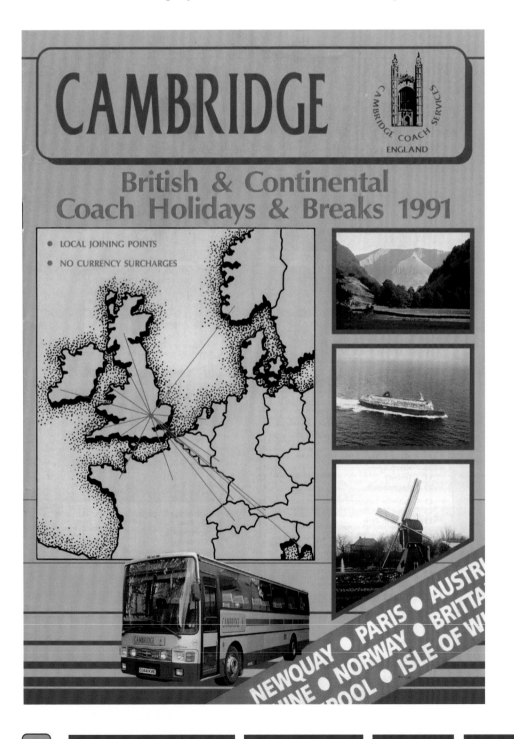

CAMBRIDGE

A brand new coach company with a wealth of experience!

On Sunday, 13th May Cambridge Coach Service commenced operation from its new depot at Ely Road, Waterbeach with a fine fleet of coaches in familiar silver and blue livery.

The company will operate the well known regular coach services to London's Airports that link Cambridge to the World. In addition Cambridge Coach Services takes over the 1990 Premier Coach Holidays and Breaks Programme and is able to provide first class coach hire facilities. Day Breaks will be operated jointly with the "New Premier".

Whilst this is a new company with a new name, many staff are already acquainted with residents and organisations of Cambridge and the surrounding area.

Please call us for all your coaching requirements, we shall be pleased to be of service.

Cambridge Coach Services Ltd
Ely Road
Waterbeach
Cambs CB5 9PG   Tel: 0223 440640

CAMBRIDGE

Arranging a coach trip? Then allow us to quote for your next outing whether it be short or long, for the day or week, in this country or abroad.

Cambridge Coach Services Ltd is the newest name in the coach business in the area, but with years of experience.

Experienced staff and drivers are available to arrange and operate any coaching requirement, backed up by a first class fleet of modern coaches in familiar blue and silver livery. Coaches for the disabled a speciality.

Hotel, ferry and theatre arrangements can all be made on your behalf.

As before we are just here to help.

Cambridge Coach
Services
Ely Road, Waterbeach
Cambridge CB5 9PG
TEL: 0223 440640

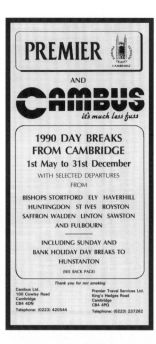

PREMIER AND CAMBUS
it's much less fuss

1990 DAY BREAKS FROM CAMBRIDGE

1st May to 31st December

WITH SELECTED DEPARTURES FROM

BISHOPS STORTFORD ELY HAVERHILL HUNTINGDON ST IVES ROYSTON SAFFRON WALDEN LINTON SAWSTON AND FULBOURN

INCLUDING SUNDAY AND BANK HOLIDAY DAY BREAKS TO HUNSTANTON

(SEE BACK PAGE)

Thank you for not smoking

Cambus Ltd.
100 Cowley Road
Cambridge
CB4 4DN
Telephone: (0223) 420544

Premier Travel Services Ltd.
King's Hedges Road
Cambridge
CB4 4PQ
Telephone: (0223) 237262

CAMBRIDGE

SUMMER HOLIDAY COACH SERVICE 72

HAVERHILL
CAMBRIDGE
ROYSTON
BALDOCK
LETCHWORTH
HITCHIN
STEVENAGE

Direct

BOURNEMOUTH

SATURDAYS ONLY
19th May until
15th September 1990

Thank you for not smoking

Cambridge Coach Services Ltd.
Ely Road
Waterbeach
Cambridge CB5 9PG
Telephone (0223) 440640

CAMBRIDGE

AUTUMN 1990   SPRING 1991

CLASSIC DAY TOURS

1st OCTOBER to 31st MAY
FROM
CAMBRIDGE

WITH SELECTED DEPARTURES FROM

BISHOPS STORTFORD   BAR HILL   ELY
HUNTINGDON   HAVERHILL   LINTON
ROYSTON   SAFFRON WALDEN
SAWSTON AND ST. IVES

THEATRE – CONCERTS
AND
SPECIAL EVENTS

Smoking is not permitted on any Coach

Cambridge Coach Services Ltd.
Ely Road
Waterbeach
Cambridge CB5 9PG
Telephone (0223) 440640

CAMBRIDGE

CLASSIC DAY TOURS

SUMMER 1991

SPECIAL OFFER
FAMILY TICKETS
SEE INSIDE FOR DETAILS

SAVE £5

FROM
CAMBRIDGE

WITH SELECTED DEPARTURES FROM LOCAL TOWNS AND VILLAGES

Smoking is not permitted on any Coach

Cambridge Coach Services Ltd.
Ely Road
Waterbeach
Cambridge CB5 9PG
Telephone (0223) 440640

INTRODUCTION

Cambridge Coach Services is probably the newest name in coaching in the Cambridge area, but, in essence, the Company can trace its origins back to Undergraduate Roadways founded in 1936.

It is with this background that I am pleased to present the Cambridge Coach Holiday and Break Brochure for 1991. Despite this year's change of operating name the Company continues to strive to improve the variety of holidays and breaks on offer. New destinations for 1991 include Norway, Brittany and the Black Forest, on the Continent of Europe, and Ireland, Llandudno and the beautiful Borders area in the British Isles.

In 1991 we have combined the Holiday and Break brochures into one in order to create a more comprehensive publication. With insurance, general information, conditions and booking form being contained in special pages at the end of the brochure for ease of reference.

I hope that after studying this brochure you will find a holiday or break which will interest you, and whether you are joining us for the first time or are a seasoned traveller with us, my staff and I look forward to welcoming you.

I N Roberts
Managing Director

Cambridge
November 1990

Cambridge Coach Services Ltd.
Ely Road
Waterbeach
Cambridge
CB5 9PG

Telephone: (0223) 440640

Photographs by courtesy of:
VARIOUS HOTELS
P & O FERRIES
CUMBRIA TOURIST BOARD
ISLE OF ARRAN TOURIST BOARD
SCOTTISH BORDERS TOURIST BOARD

PREMIER

COACH HOLIDAYS to be operated by Cambridge Coach Services

Fort William & Mull – 7 days – 13 May & 1 July – £242
Austrian Tyrol – 10 days – 22 May & 17 July – £278
Scenic Wales – 7 days – 27 May – £245
Glorious Lakeland – 7 days – 17 June & 15 July – £238
Yugoslavia – 12 days – 2 July – £326
Isle of Man – 7 days – 8 July – £260
Bude & Atlantic Coast – 7 days – 22 July – £230
Inverness & John O'Groats – 7 days – 29 July – £248
Andorra & Pyrenees – 10 days – 31 July – £315

COACH BREAKS to be operated by Cambridge Coach Services

Paris – 3 days – 19 May, 1, 16 & 29 June, 14 & 27 July – £85
Berlin – 5 days – 19 July – £197
Paris & Versailles – 4 days – 20 July & 10 August – £106
Highlights of Holland – 4 days – 27 July – £165
Edinburgh Tattoo – 4 days – 10 & 24 August – £175
Blackpool Illuminations – 3 days – every Friday from 7 September to 2 November – £66

DAY BREAKS to be operated by Premier Travel Services

Stratford-upon-Avon – Sat, 12 May – £7
Windsor – Sun 13 may – £7
Woodstock & Blenheim Palace – Thurs, 17 May – £7
York – Sat, 19 May – £8
Bath & Cheddar Gorge – Sun, 20 May – £9

Premier Travel Services Ltd
Premier Park
King's Hedges Road
Cambridge CB4 4PQ
Telephone (0223) 237262

Cambridge Coach Services
Ely Road
Waterbeach
Cambridge
CB5 9PG
TEL: 0223 440640
(as from 12th may 1990)

The cover and second page reproduced here of the A4 size 20 page 1991 brochure gives some idea of the scale of operations envisaged by Ian Roberts, including some of his own words, together with the local newspaper advertisement he used to inform the travelling public of his new company. Other items show the final separation between Premier Travel and Cambridge Coach Services, incorporating the new Waterbeach address.
(David Slater/Authors Collection)

The division of people started at the top, with Managing Director Ian Roberts assuming the same role with CCS. Fellow director David Hurry renewed his acquaintance with former Eastern Counties (EC) colleagues at CHL. In the workshops, Roy Moore stayed with PTS while Brian Kirtley took charge of maintenance at Waterbeach, assisted by David Lockwood who had joined PT as a school leaver at Haverhill, learning his trade from Jack Hitch, an experienced engineer with many years of service.

Former coach drivers who had previously been re-deployed in the garage between driving contracts also split, with Colin Malkin continuing with bodywork repairs at Kilmaine Close, while Geoff Cochrane assisted in the workshop at Waterbeach between driving duties. Traffic office staff were also separated, with Duncan Barker at Premier and Andy Gibbs at CCS. Paul Crocker, who had joined the office staff in 1989, also went to Waterbeach with CCS and was to remain with the company, pursuing a career which eventually led to management with National Express (NatEx).

Generally drivers did not have a choice, those on the NatEx rota went to PTS, along with some tour drivers. Drivers who made regular runs to the airports continued their usual routes. Some tour drivers also went to CCS with their allocated coaches initially. Brian Sellars was one and recalls operating an extended tour to Ilfracombe, departing from Premier Park as PT and returning to Waterbeach as CCS.

Disabled coach D350 KVE seen when new on Madeira Drive at Brighton (above right) in April 1987. Driver Jim Woodburn demonstrates the wheelchair lift to John Matthews, General Manager of Premier Travel Services at the time. **(Author)**

Showing the AJS inspired 'PREMIER' logo, the same coach is seen here at the 36th British Coach Rally held for the second time at Southampton Western Docks in 1990. **(Jim Woodburn Collection)**

Jim Woodburn kept his allocated coach longer than any other driver. Due to his experience with disabled passengers, going back to the early 1980s when he drove Bedford coaches with wheelchair lifts for Young's Coaches of Rampton. When Young's were acquired by PT in 1985, two Plaxton-bodied Bedfords so equipped joined the PT fleet. In the interests of standardisation, one of the batch of ten Van Hool-bodied Volvos delivered in April 1987 was fitted with a rear mounted wheelchair lift but still able to seat 53 without wheelchairs. Jim was proud of 'his' coach and drove it in the British Coach Rally at Brighton and Southampton. Due to the nature of the business, other drivers also drove 350 on express services but it was not popular, as there was less luggage space available than similar coaches due to the position of the hydraulic lift. This feature also required a fuel tank to be re-positioned, leading to the need to change over tanks on a second journey. Not all drivers remembered!

The popular service 79 to Gatwick, via Stansted and Heathrow Airports had increased to eight return journeys daily, every two hours from 0345 to 1745. In April 1989 PT had introduced a new service numbered 78, which also linked Cambridge to Heathrow and Gatwick via Harston, Royston, Baldock, Letchworth, Hitchin and Stevenage. Five return journeys on this route, timed on the alternate hours from service 79 gave an hourly service from Cambridge to Heathrow and Gatwick airports of 13 departures daily.

One week after the anticipated change of company name, E363 NEG about to depart from Waterbeach depot on an airport service still carries 'PREMIER' logos. **(David Slater)**

On Sunday 13 May 1990, the official date for separation of the companies E367 NEG, still with 'PREMIER' logos, and E361 NEG in full National Express livery are parked at the new depot at Waterbeach. **(David Slater)**

One month later about to depart on service 79 to Gatwick, E361 NEG has lost its National Express stripes and logos which have been replaced by the new company name. **(David Slater)**

The rear end of E367 NEG in Cambridge Drummer Street displays the Waterbeach address on the boot lid in July 1990. **(David Slater)**

A cross section of the formative fleet of Cambridge Coach Services at Waterbeach on Sunday 15 July 1990. Comprising a Leyland Tiger, an AEC Reliance and Volvo B10M chassis, with Plaxton and Van Hool bodies. **(David Slater)**

Premier Travel Van Hool-bodied Volvo D345 KVE loading in Cambridge Drummer Street in 1989, with another coach from the same batch of ten parked behind proves that relief coaches were often required on the busy airport services. **(John Law)**

The same coach in the same position around a year later, now sporting the Cambridge Coach Services logos. The resprayed centre off-side panel emphasises the reason why the colour silver was replaced by grey paint across the fleet. **(Richard Buckley)**

Comparison between the silver and grey paintwork can be seen here in October 1990 with E363 NEG still silver and E360 NEG, which now has grey and blue paint covering the original white. **(David Slater)**

Timetables followed the traditional Premier Travel style, with grey replacing blue as the predominant colour.

Another general view of the yard at Waterbeach revealing one coach still painted white. **(Richard Haughey)**

One of a trio of toilet equipped coaches in the new fleet about to depart from Waterbeach on 1 July 1990 on an airport service. Although D848 KVE was allocated fleet number 348 when new to Premier Travel, D846-9 KVE were registered thus to avoid confusion with AEC Reliances NEB 346-9R, although their fleet numbers were 259-62! **(Both David Slater)**

The first CCS timetable, optimistically dated 1 April 1990 showed additional 78 services serving Luton Airport, instead of Stevenage which was now served by Jetlink service 747. This was operated by Speedlink Airport Services, including two coaches provided by AJS-owned Sovereign Bus and Coach of Stevenage, for which two former PT coaches E358/9 NEG had been transferred in February 1990 and repainted in full Jetlink livery.

Repainted in Jetlink colours, 359 is seen here (left) at Central Bus Station, Heathrow Airport in August 1992. 358 can be seen back in Cambridge (right) in April 1993. **(Author`s Collection/Richard Haughey)**

Doubling the 78 frequency from five to ten return journeys gave more coaches between Cambridge and Luton than between Cambridge and Stansted, which was still served by eight departures daily. Combined routes 78/79 now gave an impressive 18 journeys each way between Cambridge, Heathrow, and Gatwick, moving towards Ian Roberts` ambition of providing a round the clock service to the airports. The slogan 'Linking Cambridge to the World' was printed on all airport timetables until 1997.

An excellent record of the transitional period between Premier Travel and Cambridge Coach Services is provided by David Slater, who drove part-time at weekends. His photos of the pair of Leyland Tigers at Haverhill bus station show VAV 254X (left) about to depart on service 38 to London at 1525 on Saturday 19 May 1990. This was the last official day of PT operation. The next year VAV 256X (right) by then adorned with the new CCS logo is seen in the same spot, operating the same journey on 9 March 1991.
(Both David Slater)

Service 38 continued to be operated by the older coaches, VAV 254X is seen here (right) on The Embankment in London, heading for Eccleston Bridge at Victoria in April 1991. AEC Reliance WEB 409T (below right) departs from Haverhill bus station for the Capital on October 1991.
(Both Trevor Brookes)

When these service 38 timetables were printed it may not have been known which company might be operating the service. Both dated to commence on 6 May 1990 it appeared to be a case of keeping all options open!

A contract with the United States Air Force (USAF) occupied a couple of coaches on a daily shuttle from the bases at RAF Mildenhall and Lakenheath to Heathrow and Gatwick airports. Originally operated by PT commencing in 1984 with one coach, the work was subject to tender and at one time also required a coach to be based at RAF Bentwaters in Suffolk. The two coaches would usually leave USAF Lakenheath together, travelling down the A11 and M11, parting company at the M25 junction for Gatwick and Heathrow respectively. One morning in July 1990 while heading for Heathrow, E364 NEG was emerging from the Epping tunnel when the actions of a car driver caused the coach to swerve, resulting in the coach overturning on to its side. Fortunately there were no serious injuries but the coach was written off after being towed back to Waterbeach, where the bodywork was stripped down.

Plaxton-bodied Volvo B10M E364 NEG suffered the indignity of returning to the Waterbeach depot on suspended lift by a MACK tow truck after overturning on the M25 Motorway in July 1990. **(Geoff Cochrane)**

Seen at Waterbeach between runs in its brief career with Cambridge Coach Services, E364 NEG retained original paintwork, not surviving long enough for grey to replace silver. **(Richard Haughey)**

Insurance claims took several months to settle and the coach was eventually written-off, while the damaged hulk remained at Waterbeach.
(David Slater)

Parked beside the wreckage of E364 NEG in September 1990 WEB 409T (left) still carries the 'PREMIER' name, proving that some time elapsed before names were changed on all coaches. By January 1991 (right) most of the bodywork had been removed in preparation for the chassis to be sold. **(Paul Hollingsbee/David Slater)**

The chassis of E364 NEG was sent to Northern Counties at Wigan to be fitted with a new Paladin 51 seat bus body to the order of Tillingbourne Valley Services, for whom it is seen operating in 1993. **(John Law)**

The newly re-bodied bus is seen here at the headquarters of Tillingbourne Valley at Cranleigh on 22 February 1992, before fleet names were applied. **(Paul Hollingsbee)**

The possibility of sending the chassis to Belgium to be re-bodied by Van Hool as a wheelchair accessible coach to supplement 350 was considered. Like many other ideas in the fledgling company the cost could not be justified and the chassis was sold to Tillingbourne Valley Services, who had it re-bodied by Northern Counties as a shorter service bus, replacing the standard six speed manual gearbox with semi-automatic transmission. The side panel which carried the company logo survived long enough to be attached to the fence at Arbury Farm, giving an indication of the new occupant. This loss of a coach resulted in several short-term vehicle hires in the form of a Plaxton-bodied Volvo and Van Hool-bodied DAF from dealer stock.

One of the coaches hired to cover the loss of the write-off was a Volvo B10M/ Plaxton Paramount 3200. Seen here on 29 September 1991, F102 HSO is in the West Ramp coach park at Heathrow. **(Trevor Brookes)**

Leyland Royal Tiger 508 DKH was a long-term hire from East Yorkshire Motor Services, seen here on the USAF contract at Holywell Row, between the RAF bases of Mildenhall and Lakenheath in September 1991. **(David Slater)**

The smallest member of the fleet was a Ford Escort Combi van, F286 NJE also carried the company logo and was used for crew changes and publicity distribution. **(David Slater)**

The letters 'SSS' shown on the destination indicator and presence of a courier indicates that D344 KVE is engaged on a tour for Spanish Speaking Services, work that had originated with the acquisition of Young's Coaches by Premier Travel in 1985. **(Author's Collection)**

Pamray Coaches from Littleport often hired coaches to Cambridge Coach Services. Berkhof-bodied Volvo GIL 4276 seen in Drummer Street ready to depart on service 78 to the airports was originally registered A60 SEV with Limebourne Coaches. **(Richard Haughey)**

Other coaching work which had passed to PT with the Young's business included tours for London based Spanish Speaking Services and transport for the supporters of Cambridge United FC. With the remaining Pye staff contracts to Fenstanton and Black Horse Drove plus a handful of school contracts, there was a constant shortage of coaches. This often led to the hire of vehicles from many other operators, such as Pamray and Storey's Coaches from Littleport, Funstons, who operated from the former PT depot at Chrishall, Kenzie's of Shepreth and Richmond's of Barley.

A pair of Plaxton Paramount 3200-bodied Volvos on hire to Cambridge Coach Services from Grey-Green Coaches seen in Drummer Street, Cambridge in August 1991. **(David Beardmore)**

Duple-bodied Volvo E893 KYW displays an array of 'On Hire' and destination stickers and was one of six Grey-Green coaches hired by CCS on 5 January 1991 **(David Slater)**

The high demand at times for coaches required on private hire often led to desperate measures by the traffic controllers, leading to many unusual hires as the express services still had to be covered on a daily basis. Part time drivers were essential, as in most coach companies to keep the wheels turning. A regular and convenient source of coaches at weekends would be Grey-Green commuter coaches, out-stationed at strategic points in Essex. A frequent occurrence on a Friday night would see any available drivers, most of whom had already completed a shift, piling into a company vehicle to tour Essex coach parks to bring Grey-Green coaches back to Cambridge. Drivers left the emergency door unlocked, with the ignition keys tucked away in the destination box to enable access.

On return to Cambridge the coach was refuelled and an early shift driver would soon be on their way to Gatwick, with a liberal array of 'On Hire to Cambridge Coach Services' and destination stickers displayed in the windows. It was usual for coaches to do two round trips to Gatwick in a day, which could lead the Grey-Green coaches to clock up more miles in two days than they did in five on their usual runs into London. The procedure was reversed on Sunday nights, to ensure the coaches were returned on time. In winter, the demisters were sometimes still warm when the Grey-Green driver commenced his duty early on a Monday morning.

Sovereign Bus and Coach at Stevenage operated few coaches but several Plaxton-bodied Leyland Tigers had found their way into the fleet by way of London Country North East through common AJS ownership. A couple, B269/82 KPF passed to PT briefly in September 1989, soon returning to Sovereign for Green Line work. B263/4 KPF from the same batch also moved around various companies in the group, appearing in several different liveries. 263 was loaned to CCS in August 1990, operating service 38 and 79. 264 made several visits to Cambridge, eventually gaining partial fleet livery in the final year of operation.

The drivers' wage structure had continued with certain elements dating back to PT days, which included 'mileage money'. This was based on 70 pence for every 100 kilometres driven loaded, which to drivers on express services could add a considerable sum to the basic pay. Commission on ticket sales was another PT tradition, based on 10% for ticket book sales and 7% for tickets issued by machine on the coach. CCS continued to pay 7% commission on all drivers' ticket sales, as at that time most tickets were sold on the coach. The coaches were fitted with Almex ticket equipment, brought down from Yorkshire in May 1988 to replace the aged manual Setrights' used by PT. Ticket books were only used as a last resort by some drivers.

Certain airport journeys were known to be busier than others, which were of course more lucrative to the driver, as they were paid commission for the fares that they took. This led to friction amongst some drivers, who liked to pick the busy runs. The wage review in October 1990 decreed that commission on ticket sales would be pooled on a daily basis by all drivers engaged on express services on any given day. The mileage element was also consolidated into an hourly rate of £3.50p, which was good at the time.

Even newspaper advertisements for staff were laid out in the traditional timetable format. This example illustrates the element of commission included in the weekly wage.

Former Young's driver Mike Dockerill poses here at Waterbeach in his allocated tour coach, D847 KVE. **(Geoff Mills)**

The AEC Reliance WEB 409T is seen on driver training duties at Royston bus station in March 1991. This coach would have been no stranger here during its eleven years in the Premier Travel fleet. Service 78 to the airports still called there until the stop was moved to the town's Tesco store in April 1992. **(Geoff Mills)**

WEB 409T and HLP 10C both attended the annual rally of the AEC Society at Nottingham in May 1991.
(Ken Worland)

Rear and side views of Harrington Grenadier-bodied AEC Reliance HLP 10C show the temporary non-standard 'CAMBRIDGE COACH SERVICES' fleet names that covered 'PREMIER TRAVEL'. **(Geoff Cochrane)**

An unusual choice for an additional coach for peak requirements came in the form of a Harrington-bodied AEC Reliance owned by Geoff Cochrane. HLP 10C was one of a pair purchased by PT from Surrey Motors in May 1974, repainted in the lighter dual blue livery which was retained on acquisition by Birds Coaches of Ongar in April 1980. Geoff was an AEC enthusiast, coming to PT from Miller Brothers of Foxton in 1979. He seized the opportunity to purchase the coach when withdrawn by Birds, with the intention of repainting it in the traditional darker blue PT livery. His plans were thwarted by the management of the day being concerned that an old coach in PT livery might affect the modern image of the company, which had taken so long to achieve.

The fact that Geoff was recently married and living in company owned accommodation at Premier Park influenced his decision to repaint the coach into Surrey Motors' livery, which it carried until circumstances changed. With encouragement from Ian Roberts the original intention was realised to wear a modified livery, reflecting the original PT company. A class VI MOT was obtained, which with the use of a CCS operator's disc enabled Geoff to hire the coach to his employers on a mileage rate basis. Of course the 'PREMIER TRAVEL' fleet names could not be displayed in PSV service, as CHL now owned the name.

With a touch of ingenuity, slip boards were created with matching gold lettering covering the 'PREMIER TRAVEL' fleet name with 'CAMBRIDGE COACH SERVICES LTD'. A spare rear name glass lettered 'CAMBRIDGE' replaced the 'PREMIER TRAVEL' name below the rear window. Geoff's primary employment with CCS was in the workshop but the availability of his coach enabled him to cover contracts and reliefs at short notice, often standing by in Drummer Street at weekends for both CCS and NatEx.

Meanwhile, Premier Park was advertised for sale in October 1990 with an asking price of £7million. Such a high valuation should have ensured that it would no longer be viable as a transport depot. PTS/CHL were due to move out by the end of the year, concentrating operations at Kilmaine Close and Cowley Road.

The 'PREMIER' name board can still be seen in 1991 on the houses used as offices at Kings Hedges Road after Cambus-owned Premier had departed and before Cambridge Coach Services moved to the site. A spur track of the Cambridgeshire guided busway now covers this spot. **(Richard Haughey)**

The year 1991 saw operations continue from Waterbeach, kept busy in January by the need to borrow six coaches from Grey-Green to enable a large contingent of Cambridge United supporters to travel to Wolverhampton during a cup run. This operation was followed by an even larger convoy of 12 coaches to Highbury in the FA Cup quarter final on 9 March, including coaches hired from many other operators. In line with updating ticketing systems it had been hoped to introduce Wayfarer machines early in 1991 but it was to be March before they were in full use. The data they generated enabled a close watch to be kept on revenue, also providing valuable statistics and indication of potential fraud.

The new coach station at Stansted Airport came into operation on the 19 March 1991, providing many coach bays, three of which were allocated to CCS. One for service 38 and one each for service 79 north and southbound. It was difficult at the time to imagine how all these bays would be occupied eventually in the future, as it would be some years before traffic built up and more new services were established.

Having left Cambridge at 1045 on 4 November 1990, D848 KVE operating service 79 pauses at the old terminal at Stansted Airport, ready to depart at 1120. The centre off-side 'continental' door denotes that a toilet and only 49 seats are fitted, unlike several others from the same batch of coaches which had 53 seats and dot-matrix destination displays.
(David Slater)

Cambridge Coach Services rule at Stansted Airport! Although the new coach station had by then been in operation for over five years, there were still many empty bays and CCS appeared to be the major operator. M306 BAV on the right had departed from Cambridge as the 0600 service 79 to Gatwick on 2 July 1996, waiting on bay 19 to continue its journey via Heathrow at 0645. N311 VAV stands on bay 18 ready to take over from the incoming service 76 from Heathrow, due to depart at 0715 to Colchester and Ipswich. The third vehicle is Ford Transit 12 seat mini-bus L515 VLK engaged on staff transfer duties.
(David Slater)

With great foresight Ian Roberts was convinced that Stansted Airport had potential for eventual expansion and continued to increase the number of coaches serving it, to ensure that CCS would become a major service provider there in the future. Service 79 provided eight departures in each direction, serving Cambridge northbound, and Heathrow and Gatwick southbound. Service 38 continued the PT timetable with four journeys each way (three on Sundays) linking Saffron Walden and Haverhill north and London southbound. From 21 April 1991 the first departure from London and the final return journey were extended to Highpoint Prison, north of Haverhill on the site of the former RAF Stradishall, which at various times had been served by the original PT route. This was to enable Londoners to visit the inmates but was not well patronised and did not feature in the timetable commencing 3 November 1991, which also reduced the frequency from four to two journeys each way daily.

As well as the airport services lots of private hires were undertaken, including continental journeys. One marathon journey was notable in many ways. The fall of Ceaucescu`s regime in Romania had led to many aid convoys making the long overland trek loaded with donated goods for the many children who had been incarcerated in awful conditions under the Dictator. This journey echoed a previous humanitarian aid expedition undertaken many years previously after the Hungarian uprising, when PT had sent a half-cab Dennis Lancet coach to Vienna in December 1956, loaded with food and clothing for the refugees as part of a United Nations convoy. It was crewed by two drivers and accompanied by Mrs Lainson, who stayed on in Vienna to help distribute the gifts donated by the people of Cambridgeshire, while PT drivers Harry Law and Bill Day returned with a load of refugees who were taken to a reception camp at Skipton in Yorkshire. The 3000 mile round trip was the first time that a PT coach had crossed the Channel but was trouble free.

In contrast, 35 years later a CCS coach driven by Brian Sellars was hired by Study Travel of Cambridge, a regular coach hire customer who had promoted a team of 22 nurses from Addenbrookes Hospital in Cambridge, under the banner 'Nurses to Romania'. Some CCS suppliers sponsored part of the cost and local publicity also helped. The Van Hool-bodied Volvo coach left Cambridge late on the night of Sunday 31 March 1991 to catch a ferry from Dover at 0200 the next morning. The rear rows of seats had been removed and a total of 92 boxes and 77 bags, not forgetting two pairs of crutches, three prams and a wheelchair were somehow packed into every available space. There were concerns that the coach was overloaded but a quick trip to a local weighbridge ensured that the total load including passengers was legal.

A feeder driver took the coach down to Dover, giving the two man crew a full days` driving across Europe to an overnight stop near Vienna. Bob Janes, the co-driver flew back from Vienna to Heathrow the next day, where he no doubt was easily able to find a connecting coach to take him back to Cambridge. The medical staff on board from Addenbrookes Hospital spent ten days working in local hospitals, distributing the items brought with them in the city of Arad. It made sense to have just one driver on the final lap of the journey, which gave Brian Sellars a well-earned break on arrival. The return journey was taken in the same stages, with a co-driver flying out to Vienna to meet the returning party.

Back on the right road, the search for fuel completed, we head for the Romanian border.

Part of a ten page album presented to driver Brian Sellars by the nurses he took to Romania. **(Brian Sellars)**

Life within Blazefield after Premier Travel and Cambridge Coach Services. VAV 254X (left) entering Leeds bus station with Yorkshire Coastliner in April 1992. Re-registered HIL 9374 (right) with Rover at Bromsgrove in February 1994. **(Peter Hirst/David Cole)**

VAV 256X wore both Harrogate Independent Travel 'Challenger' livery (left) at the 1992 Showbus rally at Woburn Abbey and Ingfield Northern Rose colours seen (right) at Settle on 22 November 1994. **(Richard Haughey/Paul Hollingsbee)**

While still based at Waterbeach, the coach fleet fluctuated within the group. The pair of X-reg Leyland Tigers went north in July 1991. VAV 254X eventually entered the Yorkshire Coastliner fleet, while sister VAV 256X gained Harrogate Independent Travel livery after both being operated in full CCS livery. Loans in the opposite direction included an East Yorkshire Leyland Royal Tiger in September 1991, used mainly on the USAF contract from RAF Mildenhall to Heathrow Airport. AEC Reliance WEB 409T went back and forth between Rover Coaches and CCS several times, with various Rover coaches in exchange. The most long-term transfer being a former Wallace Arnold Y-reg Plaxton-bodied Volvo re-registered TXI 6342 by Rover, soon gaining CCS fleet names and registration YIJ 387 to match its allocated fleet number.

New to Wallace Arnold Tours as FUA 393Y and re-registered TXI 6342 by Rover Coaches in May 1991. Seen here in service with Cambrdge Coach Services (left) in March and (right) August 1992, after it gained registration YIJ 387, eventually returning to Rover Coaches at Bromsgrove as seen on page 40. **(Ken Worland/David Beardmore)**

Most of the Van Hool fleet were replaced by four Plaxton Paramount 3500-bodied Volvos (G95-8 RGG) from the Parks of Hamilton fleet in an effort to upgrade the front line coaches. An advantage of Parks` specification was that the centrally mounted toilet could be replaced by two pairs of double seats to increase the capacity to 53, giving more flexible operation. The first of these, G95 RGG spent a couple of summer seasons on loan to associated Rover Coaches, carrying their logo to meet their peak tour requirements.

Two of the four Plaxton Paramount 3500-bodied coaches acquired from Parks of Hamilton are seen here in August 1992. Although ticket machines are fitted, G96 RGG has no destination blind yet. **(Paul Hollingsbee)**

The Canadian War Memorial at Vimy Ridge in France makes an impressive backdrop as G98 RGG pauses on the way to Paris while operating one of many tours to the French Capital. **(Ken Worland)**

G95 RGG spent its first two summers with Rover at Bromsgrove. Seen on a brief visit to Cambridge carrying the 'ROVER COACHES' name, the Cambridge Coach Services logo would eventually be applied and the coach would re-visit Bromsgrove while operating service 71. **(Chris Moody)**

Rover Coaches were an old established operator, started in the 1920`s with a Rover six seater limousine, hence the fleet name. In February 1989 the Brown family sold Rover to David Stevenson, a former Midland Red manager who had wide experience with many other bus and coach companies. The newly formed company, Rover Coaches (Bromsgrove) Ltd expanded rapidly, venturing into stage carriage services as well as continuing with traditional coach hire and operating services for NatEx. K&M Travel were acquired in March 1990, giving Rover a second base in Worcester managed by former owner Mike Key. Operational requirements also led to exchanges between the CCS and Rover fleets.

On the 9 November 1991, one month after being made redundant from the factory that I had worked in since leaving AJS owned PTS, I had a phone call from CCS at Waterbeach asking if I fancied driving a coach to Gatwick. My initial reaction was that my wife had gone shopping in our car, so I had no transport, which brought the reply "I'll pick you up then". I drove E361 NEG on the 1045 service 79 from Cambridge to Gatwick, via Stansted and Heathrow, visiting Terminal 4 for the first time. The return journey was the 1445 service 78 to Cambridge via Heathrow and Luton airports. On return to Cambridge, I left the coach in Drummer Street for another driver to take back to Gatwick on the next departure and rode home to Burwell on the 1820 Cambus service 111. I earned £7 commission on top of the £3.50p an hour that day, despite not selling any tickets.

This was my first involvement with CCS and the first of many journeys to Gatwick via Heathrow and Stansted or Luton airports. I already had a couple of other part-time jobs, one working in a local garage, the other driving when needed by DJ Coaches at nearby Fordham. I enjoyed the experience of driving express coaches more than school contracts or private hire but the conditions at Waterbeach and the distance from home did not impress me at the time.

Caught by the camera in the coach park at Gatwick Airport, the author is busy completing his paperwork before commencing the return journey to Cambridge. **(Chris Moody)**

The author's first journey for Cambridge Coach Services was on 9 November 1991, driving Plaxton-bodied Volvo E361 NEG, seen here in Drummer Street on another occasion. **(Ken Worland)**

A familiar scene at Gatwick South Terminal to any driver operating late shifts was the sight of one coach ready to depart from stop eight as they arrived at stop nine, when both were running on time. **(Both David Slater)**

Chapter 3 RETURN TO CAMBRIDGE

By the time I called to collect my wages on the 25 November 1991, Cambridge Coach Services (CCS) had moved back to the former Premier Park at Kings Hedges Road in Cambridge. This seemed like 'coming home' to me, leading to several more shifts throughout the winter. Nobody was surprised that travellers had broken into the secure premises while it was unoccupied, even less surprised to find how they had left it, after availing themselves of the facilities and salvaging anything of scrap value. The automatic coach wash had suffered badly in this respect, unable to function throughout the winter, although efforts were made to repair it, some parts were difficult to obtain. The nature of the lease from the owners meant that no office buildings were available. Three Portakabins arranged in a horseshoe shape and linked internally provided cramped but sufficient accommodation for the slimmed down administration staff and driver`s locker room, incorporating clock-on and pay-in facilities.

The return to the former Premier Park site in Cambridge was a welcome move for everyone at Cambridge Coach Services, especially the eventual re-instatement of the automatic coach wash. Plaxton -bodied Volvo E365 NEG receives the treatment here. **(All Chris Moody)**

The original workshops built by Percival`s and previously utilised by Premier Travel (PT) for running repairs were re-activated, coping with the requirements of a busy fleet of coaches. The extensive hard-standing laid down by PT as part of their master plan was not all required, so the far end was sub-let to various other companies from time to time. For instance the contractors engaged by Cambridge Cable, now known as Virgin Media were laying miles of cables across the county at the time and parked their vehicles there overnight, storing large quantities of cable and ducting which was used on a daily basis.

East Anglian Driver Training also made use of the yard, which was usually almost empty throughout the day for initial manoeuvring practice with their HGV and PSV pupils. This link proved to be of mutual benefit, as several of their pupils took on driving positions with CCS. Some of the instructors also helped out with driving duties, especially the 1800 Gatwick duty, on which the driver usually returned as a passenger.

Blazefield Holdings Ltd had been formed earlier in 1991 by Giles Fearnley and Stuart Wilde to acquire the bus companies but not the property interests of AJS Holdings, of which they had both been directors. Alan Stephenson retaining a minority holding in Blazefield, whilst Giles and Stuart also retained minority interests in AJS Holdings. For a time CCS was the only operating company owned by AJS Holdings but under the control of Sovereign Buses (Harrow) as caretakers, although Ian Roberts remained Managing Director. Speedlink Airport Services, then part of Drawlane, had been keen to add the CCS airport routes to their network for some time. In the event no offer was forthcoming, so it would be almost a decade before the inevitable happened, although under much different circumstances. In November 1991 CCS was purchased by Blazefield from AJS to become part of Sovereign Bus and Coach Companies Stevenage operations within Blazefield Holdings.

Ian Roberts did not enjoy good health, having undergone a kidney transplant and suffered minor heart attacks. This was not helped by the intense strain of controversial management within the original PT company, combined with fighting off the advances of Cambus Holdings Ltd (CHL) twice, with only limited success the second time. I remember him being taken from his office at Premier Park to hospital by ambulance one morning while still working for PT. The months of uncertainty following the formation of CCS seemed more settled once the operation had returned to Premier Park, which had reverted to the original address of Arbury Farm to distance the company from the name Premier.

Staff Bulletins resumed late in January 1992, with Ian stating how pleased he was to be back at work after sickness, thanking staff for their support over the previous eight weeks of his absence. He hoped to progress from half days to full-time over the next few weeks, although the Cambridge Omnibus Society reported in their magazine that he had been unable to speak at their meeting on 10 March, due to ill health.

Mixed identity shows E365 NEG lettered for both Sovereign and Jetlink while in service with Cambridge Coach Services (left) labelled with 'On-Hire' stickers unloading passengers in Emmanuel Street, Cambridge on 28 August 1992. Two weeks earlier the same coach can be seen in Luton (right) while operating Jetlink 747 service to Heathrow and Gatwick airports.
(Richard Haughey/M.A.Penn)

Transfers of coaches continued, with E365 NEG loaned to Sovereign at Stevenage in January for several months as back-up for similar 358/9 on Jetlink work. The CCS logos were replaced by Sovereign names in blue lower case vinyl, later changed to large white Jetlink 747 lettering applied to the front panel and the first blue stripe on either side. Operational requirements sometimes led to a temporary return to Cambridge, pressed into service with 'On Hire to CCS' stickers, despite the grey/blue livery. Combined with the appearance at the depot of 358/9 for maintenance, both in full Jetlink livery there were strong rumours and speculation that Speedlink, parent of Jetlink had taken over CCS. This was also compounded by the sight of a Speedlink coach regularly parked overnight at Arbury Farm. The facts were that Sovereign operated part of Jetlink 747 under contract to Speedlink and Speedlink operated an 098 National Express (NatEx) journey from London that terminated in Huntingdon, parking at Arbury Farm by mutual arrangement.

The short term transfer of coaches between Blazefield companies kept Algar Signcraft busy, they were an established local company that had previously supplied vinyl lettering and signs to PT and continued to give excellent service to the new company. Initially 'CAMBRIDGE' appeared in place of the name 'PREMIER' beside the King`s College Chapel logo on the front and sides of coaches. To give a greater impact this was replaced by the full company title in large capital letters in Friz Quadrata typeface on the front and rear of coaches. The former Parks of Hamilton coaches were the first to receive this style, followed by all further acquisitions and the other coaches in the fleet were updated during 1992. Small fleet numbers were carried below the front windscreen and rear windows, also adjacent to fuel fillers but seldom referred to. Individual identities were introduced to each coach by naming them after Cambridge University colleges, with the appropriate college crest being carried in blue vinyl either side of the fleet name on the front of the coach.

The original company logo contrasts with the full 'CAMBRIDGE COACH SERVICES' fleet name. **(Both David Slater)**

A pair of Plaxton Paramount 3500-bodied Volvo B10Ms fitted with toilets were acquired by Blazefield towards the end of the year. New to Bleanch of Hetton-le-Hole, they had run on contract to NatEx from the North East, arriving in plain white. F884 RFP joined the CCS fleet in white, gaining grey/blue and numbered 388 by February 1992.

Pressed into service in plain white, F884 RFP awaits its next duty in January 1992. **(Ken Worland)**

Sister coach F885 RFP was also used by Rover Coaches in plain white before gaining fleet livery in April 1992. Seen here leaving Coventry in June 1992 operating a National Express journey. **(Paul Hollingsbee)**

Six months later, F884 RFP had been repainted and fitted with destination blinds but still retained its full windscreen as seen here in Drummer Street about to depart for Gatwick Airport.
(David Beardmore)

F885 RFP went to Rover, running in white, often on hire to NatEx until repainted grey/blue in April 1992 and given fleet number 349. It was also used at Cambridge with Rover names. In fact I drove it to Gatwick on 25 September 1992 as F885 RFP. 349 was re-registered YXI 2749 by Rover, but reverted to original registration soon after joining the CCS fleet on the demise of Rover Coaches. Both coaches were eventually fitted with destination boxes and split windscreens, in line with most other coaches in the fleet.

Drastic changes to service 38 commenced on 23 February 1992. The northern terminus was changed from Haverhill to Cambridge Drummer Street, increasing the running time from 2 hours 35 minutes to 3 hours. The long detour into Stansted Airport where crew changes were undertaken was also dropped. With the opening of new facilities in Bulleid Way, overseen by Green Line, the southern terminus was moved round the corner from Eccleston Bridge to stop seven in Buckingham Palace Road. Layover bays were available on Bulleid Way for coaches that displayed a Green Line Associated Service sign inside the windscreen.

Another innovation introduced in April was a dozen electronic swipe machines to enable credit card transactions to be carried out on coaches for passengers' convenience. Being battery operated they were soon dubbed 'PDQ's' but were not always so 'quick'. In some instances they saved time by not requiring large amounts of change to be found by the driver. A constant problem was newly arrived visitors to England presenting a £20, sometimes even a £50 note for what then was a £12 fare from Heathrow, (£14 from Gatwick) to Cambridge. Some drivers were reluctant to use them, as they could take time to operate, especially when the batteries were low. Accepting the wrong type of card or other errors in operation could lead to a waybill discrepancy, this could result in a deduction from wages, which was not popular.

Loading in Cambridge, bound for Oxford on service 75 is F425 DUG in June 1993. **(David Beardmore)**

As E365 NEG passes through High Wycombe on a late service 75 journey to Oxford, the bus station is almost deserted, apart from the local Wycombe Bus Company buses parked overnight. **(Chris Moody)**

Further expansion commenced on 26 April 1992 with the introduction of a new service numbered 75 between Cambridge and Oxford via Stansted Airport, marketed as 'The Inter Varsity Link'. The route out of Cambridge diverted along Hills Road serving a bus stop adjacent to Addenbrooke's Hospital, calling at Stansted Airport and High Wycombe bus station. The route into Oxford was via Headington and Headley Way, serving a bus stop close to the John Radcliffe Infirmary.

Having commenced his career in the City of Oxford, Ian Roberts was aware of the potential patronage, so promoted the new service as 'Linking two of this country's Principal Teaching Hospitals'. Four daily return journeys were scheduled with a running time of 2 hours 40 minutes and an extra five minutes between Stansted and Cambridge on return journeys. The timings were devised to slot in between the service 79 departures, giving virtually an hourly service during the day between Stansted Airport and Cambridge. A pair of former Wallace Arnold 'low-drive' coaches joined the fleet mainly to operate this service, registered F424/5 DUG initially numbered 389/90.

An additional early morning journey at 0200 numbered 77 from Cambridge to Gatwick Airport, calling only at Stansted via the Dartford Crossing with a reduced running time of two hours was also introduced on 26 April. This enabled an earlier return journey from Gatwick at 0645 operating as service 79 via Heathrow and Stansted. The North Terminal at Gatwick which had opened in March 1988 was also served from that date. On service 78 the stop at Royston was moved from the town's bus station to a new stop adjacent to the recently opened Tesco supermarket, closer to the A505 road, reducing running times.

At the same time as the new timetables were introduced, an excess charge of £1 per item for more than two cases per passenger and £5 for dogs (except guide dogs), packaged cycles and skis also came into force. This proved to be controversial, causing the charge for dogs to be reduced to £1 and skis to £2 by the end of the year. It would be four years before the cycle charge was also reduced to £2. There was often controversy regarding the term 'packaged' between drivers and passengers, particularly with students travelling between Oxford and Cambridge. Now in the twenty-first century the frequent Stagecoach service X5 drivers remain seated, raising the side lockers automatically, oblivious to luggage being loaded by passengers, or how unpackaged cycles could damage other luggage.

Van Hool-bodied Volvo B490 UNB of Rover Coaches is seen in Drummer Street on hire to Cambridge Coach Services in June 1992. **(Richard Haughey)**

E366 NEG can be seen (left) in Cambridge Drummer Street at the start of its journey, and (right) at the final destination, the upper departure level at Gatwick North Terminal. **(David Beardmore/Chris Moody)**

The extra services and continued volume of Private Hire, Classic Day Tours and Holiday Tours ensured a constant shortage of coaches, met by extensive hiring in of Volvos, Tigers and even an AEC from Premier/Cambus, also DAFs from Whippet, some on a self-drive basis, as CCS had many part time drivers available. Other vehicles came from within Blazefield in the form of a unique Wadham Stringer-bodied Volvo B57 and a Leyland Lynx from Sovereign which were often used on service 38 to London at weekends. Various coaches from the Rover fleet were also borrowed, but at least they carried the same grey/blue livery as CCS vehicles.

On 1 July a notice was posted announcing that the Chairman and Board of Directors had appointed Roger Birch to the position of Operations' Supervisor. He had joined CCS as a driver, after previous experience with Eastern Counties (EC), Ambassador Travel and PT. Having undertaken administration and revenue protection duties for some time and generally assisting with the running of the company it was regarded as a formality. The notice reminded drivers that they were required to comply with his instructions, giving Roger their full support and co-operation. This appointment confirmed Ian Roberts' commitment to promote up through the ranks, a policy that was to continue throughout the history of the company which would lead to management for Roger.

School contracts were not renewed in September 1992, resulting in changes to certain drivers` duties. An arrangement was made with Whippet Coaches to cover some of their commitments in the Linton area in exchange for the Philips (former Pye) staff contract from Fenstanton to Cambridge, reducing dead mileage for both operators. Also recorded in September, coach number 351 broke down in Oxford while operating service 75. City of Oxford Motor Services provided a replacement coach in the form of a Duple-bodied Leyland Leopard, which continued to maintain the service for several days until 351 had been repaired. The appearance of this coach in Cambridge soon sparked rumours that service 75 was to become a joint operation!

Towards the end of the year, it was decided to locate a spare driver at Gatwick, initially on Mondays and Fridays, when traffic delays were worst but it eventually became a daily duty, known as the 'shunt'. The allocated driver would ride down as a passenger on an early coach, enabling a prompt return if there were delays on the outward journey, which there invariably were. Throughout the day there was always a driver who had taken their legal break ready to take over an arriving coach for an immediate return if necessary. This system enabled departure reliability from Gatwick to improve considerably.

Very few people carried a mobile phone in those days, as they were not yet compact enough to fit the average pocket. Due to their size and weight they were then known as the 'brick', an early example was required to be carried by the 'shunt' driver to maintain contact between the coach park at Gatwick and the traffic office in Cambridge. The usual method of communication between coaches continued with two-way radios, which had been introduced by PT and adopted by many local operators allowing coach to coach contact which helped to avoid delays, particularly on congested motorways. Messages could also be 'patched through' to home base by other base stations over longer distances. The last 'shunt' driver would usually drive back the 2200 service 79 coach to Cambridge, with the incoming driver as passenger. This made the 1800 duty from Cambridge a popular one, with a ride back on the cushions.

November 1 saw the registering of the route of service 75 between Chorleywood and Oxford. Instead of continuing round the M25 to junction 16 to join the M40 motorway and diverting in to High Wycombe, the revised route left the M25 at junction 18 to serve new stops at Chorleywood, Little Chalfont and Amersham Old Town, before serving High Wycombe bus station as previously. Then following the A40 through West Wycombe to Stokenchurch, where another new stop was established at the Kings Arms, before joining the M40 at junction five to continue to Oxford. After serving stops at Thornhill Park & Ride, Headington, Headley Way and Summertown the bus station at Gloucester Green was reached, continuing to the Pear Tree service area where the route terminated. These additional stops added another 15 minutes to running times but were supported by both Buckinghamshire and Oxfordshire County Councils. Additional student passengers were gained for both Cambridge and Oxford destinations, as well as local passengers in and out of High Wycombe. In return for assistance given by the local Oxford and Wycombe Bus Companies it was agreed to offer free travel to their employees between High Wycombe and Oxford on production of their staff pass.

Meanwhile in the West Midlands, Rover Coaches were struggling, leading to Blazefield Holdings taking a financial interest. At some point in 1992 a new company was registered as Associated Bus & Coach Investments Ltd (trading as Rover Coaches), becoming a Blazefield subsidiary.

The recent face-lift of AEC Reliance WEB 409T in 1992 shows the revised fleet name and Churchill College crests on the new front panel below the windscreen and additional grey paint around the destination glass.
(Richard Haughey)

Now on its second visit from Rover and fitted with destination blinds, YIJ 387 arrives back in Cambridge in June 1993, sporting the Churchill College crest taken from WEB 409T on its departure. **(Paul Hollingsbee)**

January 1993 saw the sale of the solitary AEC Reliance WEB 409T to a Welsh operator, followed by the transfer for the second season of Volvo YIJ 387 from Rover Coaches in exchange for G95 RGG, needed to operate Rover's tours. An unusual vehicle arrived in March painted white. Initially numbered 392, K392 FEG was an 18-seat Toyota Optimo midi-coach which was repainted in full fleet livery before entering service on private hire, tour feeders and lightly loaded services. A Wayfarer ticket machine was also fitted and a crew seat at the front made it useful for crew changes at Drummer Street and taking drivers route learning on new services. A third ex Wallace Arnold 'low-drive' coach arrived in March. F421 DUG was repainted and entered service on 2 April as fleet number 391.

The Optimo midi-coach parked inside Drummer Street bus station on 19 April 1994 awaiting a space to load for the 1730 service 70 to Birmingham. **(David Slater)**

Approaching Drummer Street on 1 March 1995, the Optimo can be seen driven by the author on a crew change, as he took over the 1200 service 79 to Gatwick Airport. **(Trevor Brookes)**

The third 'low-drive' Plaxton Paramount 3200 coach to arrive from Wallace Arnold was F421 DUG, seen passing the War Memorial in Saffron Walden in October 1994 on the way to London on service 38. **(David Beardmore)**

Another internal transfer saw the CCS fleet names on 360 replaced by Jetlink vinyls in blue and the words 'inter airport' below accompanied by the red outline of an aircraft in the style carried by fully liveried Jetlink coaches. Strangely the King's College logo remained on the boot lid while the coach was allocated to Stevenage, enabling the return to Cambridge of 365. To add further confusion, 360 also operated airport services from Cambridge so adorned! A few months later the controversial Jetlink logos would be removed and 360 would join 359 with Rover at Bromsgrove, where to add to its identity crisis it sometimes carried both Cambridge and Rover fleet names at the same time as can be seen on page 40.

The temporary 'Jetlink' lettering applied to E360 NEG also reveals the 'SOVEREIGN BUSES (HARROW) LTD, T/A CAMBRIDGE COACH SERVICES' legal lettering carried by all coaches at the time, as well as the King's College Chapel logo on the boot lid. **(Both Algar Signcraft)**

During 1993 alterations at Drummer Street bus station resulted in express coach departures moving to temporary stops at Parkside, where E360 NEG can be seen in service with Cambridge Coach Services, despite the Jetlink lettering. **(Richard Haughey)**

Timetable changes introduced on 16 May 1993 saw increased running time on service 75, terminating at Oxford Bus Station instead of proceeding to the service area. In response to public demand, an additional stop was introduced at Hazlemere, between Amersham and High Wycombe. The Imperial War Museum at Duxford was also served for a trial period by a short diversion from junction 10 of the M11 on the first journey from Oxford, and the 1715 return journey from Cambridge. Other additional stops to affect services 75/78/79 were a brave attempt to co-ordinate coach and train travel. The stop at Cambridge Rail Station was introduced due to the withdrawal of direct trains from Cambridge to Stansted Airport and entailed changing service 78/79 coach departure times from Drummer Street from quarter to the hour to on the hour, with subsequent arrival and return departure times at Heathrow and Gatwick also being due on the hour. A detour from the M25 motorway between junctions 19 and 20 calling at a bus stop at Langleybury Church on the A41 trunk road offered connections with local buses to Watford and Hemel Hempstead.

For a trial period during the summer of 1993 coaches called at Cambridge Rail Station. G98 RGG passes a Cambus Optare City Pacer operating the 'City Rail Link' on 2 August. **(Paul Carter)**

E365 NEG waits at the bus stop at Langleybury Church, a short diversion from the M25 motorway on the way to Oxford. **(Chris Moody)**

The first former Wallace Arnold Plaxton Paramount 3500 coach to join the fleet was H629 UWR in December 1993, seen here at Drummer Street in May 1995. **(David Beardmore)**

The Sprite caravan seen here at Arbury Farm arrived on 9 August 1993. **(Richard Haughey)**

An even more unusual arrival in August was a Sprite caravan in full fleet livery complete with CCS logos. This fleet addition carried no passengers but served several purposes, mainly in publicity and promotion of services, particularly at the launch of new routes at various events and local markets. It also proved useful as a mobile office on occasions such as major rail replacement services carried out by Sovereign Bus and Coach. Ian Roberts was keen to exploit any opportunity to promote his company and hand-outs bearing the familiar logo were commissioned in the form of mugs, coasters, pens and even carrier bags, which were issued to passengers on shopping excursions examples of which can be seen on page 96. An opportunity was missed on these lines with the provision of aircraft style sick bags which were freely available on coaches, as these were supplied in plain white!

Although the stop at Cambridge Rail Station was popular with some passengers, traffic congestion and late running caused delays at certain times of the day. Very often a driver would be kept waiting at Drummer Street to take over the inward coach for the next departure, resulting in the station stop being removed from the timetable from 31 October for operational reasons. This date also saw service 75 departure and arrival times change to on the hour. On the odd occasion when coaches were running to time, four CCS coaches could be seen at the bus stop at Langleybury Church, 75 and 78 northbound and southbound.

The 'shared spare' coach, E358 NEG carried various combinations of fleet name as seen (left) leaving Drummer Street bus station and (right) entering Luton bus station on Jetlink service 747 from Stevenage to Gatwick. **(David Beardmore/M.A. Penn)**

David Hurry left Cambus-owned Premier Travel Services (PTS) in September 1993, moving to a position with Sovereign at Stevenage. The management of Sovereign went shopping at Volvo dealer Yeates of Loughborough in December 1993, purchasing a trio of consecutively numbered former Wallace Arnold coaches with Plaxton Paramount 3500 bodies. H627/8 UWR were re-painted in Jetlink livery and numbered 327/8 to replace E358/9 NEG at Stevenage. As CCS was placed under Sovereign Bus & Coach management within Blazefield Holdings, a common fleet numbering system was adopted, resulting in the third coach H629 UWR being numbered 329 in the CCS fleet and carrying the grey/blue livery. 358 was repainted white with blue skirt panels and allocated as a 'shared spare' between Sovereign and CCS, wearing a varied combination of either or both fleet names at times. 359 was sent to Rover at Bromsgrove and repainted in standard CCS style grey/blue, but may never have carried the CCS logo, as ROVER fleet names were applied, along with similar 360 from the CCS fleet in January 1994. It is, however included in the fleet list.

In January 1994 the group fleet numbering system required coaches 383-6 to be re-numbered 395-8 and 388-91 became 384/24/5/1 in line with the last two digits of their registration numbers. K392 FEG became 492 and Rover 392 was re-numbered 374. When not required by Sovereign or CCS, 358 would sometimes replace failed National Express (NatEx) coaches. Although it had carried full NatEx livery from new until becoming a Jetlink coach, the new mainly white livery fitted the bill, apart from the blue skirt panels. At lunchtime on 10 February 1994 Andy Gibbs phoned me to see if I was available to work, "The service 305 coach has broken down on its way from Southend, can you run the service up to Digbeth, while they send a replacement coach down from Liverpool?" When I agreed, he said that he would send 358 to Drummer Street to load the passengers and bring the coach up to the depot for me to take over. Despite running late, I was able to cover the full route, as I had done many times previously with PT. On arrival at Digbeth Coach Station in Birmingham I transferred the onward passengers to the waiting coach bound for Liverpool. I was also recognised by a former Midland Red Inspector from my PT days before taking a legal break and returning empty to Cambridge. One month later, the same coach was seen heading for Bristol on service 747, covering for another failed NatEx coach.

Toyota Optimo 18-seater K392 FEG often had sufficient capacity to operate service 70 between Cambridge and Birmingham, en-route at Pool Meadow bus station in Coventry in 1994. **(Paul Carter Collection)**

After two summers as a Cambridge coach, YIJ 387 returned to Bromsgrove in October 1993, re-gaining the ROVER name. Here resting in Cambridge between service 70 duties. **(Chris Moody)**

As service 70 was operated jointly by Cambridge Coach Services and Rover Coaches, both names were carried on E360 NEG for a time, showing how closely together they operated. **(David Beardmore)**

On 23 March 1994 I was one of several drivers who rode in the Optimo midi-coach to learn a new route to Birmingham. The long awaited M1 – A1 link road was nearing completion, which was expected to reduce the travelling time between Cambridge and Birmingham by up to 30 minutes. CCS hoped to establish a new service avoiding the traditional route via Bedford and Northampton, which was then part of the NatEx network. The new service numbered 70, commenced on 27 March with four return journeys daily and a running time of three hours. Coaches departed from both Cambridge and Birmingham at 0830, 1230, 1730 and 2130. Intermediate stops were at Girton Corner, Huntingdon, Thrapston, Wicksteed Park, Kettering, Coventry and Birmingham Airport, terminating in the Bull Ring bus station at Birmingham. Two round trips each were operated by CCS and Rover Coaches from Bromsgrove, who were by then closely associated with CCS under common ownership within Blazefield Holdings. The joint operation of service 70 also enabled frequent transfers between the two fleets with a reduction in dead mileage. At first 359/60 were allocated to run from Bromsgrove, travelling empty to and from Birmingham.

At first the extra journey time allowed was taken up by travelling on existing roads via Rothwell and Market Harborough until the last section of the A14 opened in July. NatEx soon introduced a similar route, numbered 314 utilising the new link road and including its designation in the route number, with departures from Cambridge at 0800, 1200 and 1600 in addition to their three existing service 305 departures at 0905, 1305 and 1705. Combined with the four CCS journeys, this gave a total of ten coaches a day between Cambridge and Birmingham. Naturally this was unsustainable, resulting in CCS withdrawing service 70 on expiry of the published timetable on 29 October. Without the competition, CCS might have built up a viable service but many journeys were lightly loaded. I drove the route 27 times, with 17 different coaches, the most frequent one being the 18 seat-Optimo, although the most passengers I carried was 27 on the 1730 from Cambridge to Birmingham one evening.

Over a period of time NatEx also reduced the number of journeys until none operated via the A14, which had become very congested, with frequent delays. The service 314 continued with variations between Cambridge and Birmingham, and an extension north to Southport as part of the NatEx network. Significantly the Friday and Sunday afternoon return journey between Cambridge and Birmingham, that traced its roots back to PT service 5, continued until March 2012 as a short 314 working. Operated in turn by Cambus, NatEx-owned operations and Burtons Coaches, for whom I drove it 112 times between November 2006 and August 2009 in a variety of coaches, including fellow TGM companies Classic and Excel vehicles although a Burtons NatEx-liveried coach was used when available.

After two seasons as a Rover coach, G95 RGG had regained Cambridge Coach Services names when seen in 1994 at Birmingham International Airport on service 70, heading towards the City Centre. **(Chris Moody)**

The Rover coach shown on page 33 as F885 RFP was re-registered YXI 2749 in March 1993. Seen here loading for service 70 to Birmingham in the entrance to Drummer Street on 22 October 1994. **(David Slater)**

This Berkhof Esprite- bodied Volvo had started life as B592 XNO in the fleet of The King's Ferry. First operated by Rover in plain white and re-registered TXI 5497 in July 1991 it then transferred to Northern Rose, whose livery it retained on return to Rover while operating service 70 to Cambridge on 24 June 1994, identifed by a magnetic 'CAMBRIDGE COACH SERVICES' fleet name. **(David Beardmore)**

New to Parks of Hamilton, E586 UHS was re-registered YXI 2748 with fleet number 393 by Rover Coaches in March 1993. Seen here at the Mildenhall Air Show on 28 May 1993, a few weeks later the author drove it to Gatwick in service on hire to Cambridge Coach Services on one of its short-term loans. This coach is not included in the fleet list, being sold in February 1995, three months before the demise of Rover. **(David Slater)**

Other changes in 1994 saw the revision of the seasonal Saturday service 72 to Bournemouth start from Cambridge instead of Haverhill, where it had traditionally been operated from the PT depot by driver Joe Gogin. When Joe retired, he was replaced by Mick Sheppard, a regular part-time driver who continued with CCS. The option was also available to serve Heathrow Airport if required to give extra capacity on what then were busy summer Saturdays. As I was then working more days for CCS than my other part-time jobs, I decided that I would be better off as a full-time driver with them and drove my last Premier/Cambus coach on 15 April, joining the CCS drivers` rota on 30 May. I had already learned the airport routes, services 38 to London and 75 to Oxford and driven the Optimo midi-coach on four different private hires. This proved to be the right decision, as less than two years later Stagecoach acquired Cambus.

After leaving Haverhill at 0800, Van Hool -bodied Volvo D351 KVE is about to depart from Cambridge at 0845 on 29 August 1992 on service 72 to Bournemouth. **(David Beardmore)**

Seen resting after arrival at Bournemouth Transport Interchange, Plaxton-bodied Volvo F424 DUG had also operated service 72. **(Raymond Smith)**

Although I preferred the regular service work, I was not keen on early morning starts. Once I found my place on the drivers` rota and studied the shift patterns, I was able to work out which other drivers could swap duties with me, enabling me to work mainly late shifts, which I preferred. There were several drivers who preferred early starts and finishes. So long as they were allocated the same rest day as myself, it was easy to arrange a mutual duty change for the whole week, which suited us both.

Ford Transit minibus L281 LNK took staff to Brighton on 23 April 1995 to support the crew of M307 BAV, which was entered in the British Coach Rally that year (page 48). **(Author`s Collection)**

Rear view of Ford Transit, parked in Drummer Street while engaged on a crew-change shows the towbar used to pull the company caravan to events. **(David Slater)**

Another former Wallace Arnold coach, G519 LWU joined the fleet in May, followed by the news that no less than eight brand new coaches had been ordered for delivery in the autumn. In the meantime, a useful small addition was an eight-seat Ford Transit Tourneo finished in full fleet livery, registered L281 LNK and allocated fleet number 881. A towbar was fitted to pull the company caravan to various locations for promotional work, in-between these duties it was kept busy on crew changes, tour feeders and publicity distribution work. The Oxford service 75 was proving successful, requiring reliefs at peak times such as Friday and Sunday evenings, when students would be travelling home or between the two University cities.

With frequent shortages of coaches, it was usual to hire in from other operators. On Friday 27 May I found myself acting as conductor on a Richmond`s coach taking fares on the 1700 service 75 from Cambridge to Oxford, returning at 2100. The 57 seats were all occupied by the time we left Cambridge, calling at Stansted Airport to drop off and pick up more passengers. As there was no Wayfarer ticket machine on the hired coach, I had to write out all the tickets in a ticket book, most passengers requiring returns for the weekend. I remember passing the water tower in between the M11 and Harlow before I had finished collecting all the fares, and able to take a seat.

By the end of July, I was enjoying all the benefits of pooled commission on daily ticket sales, which could be up to £30 at weekends. One week my share of commission totalled £86.50 for 43 hours over five days` work, hardly representative of the number of tickets sold on my late turns. I also calculated that I would have had to work 74 hours for Premier/ Cambus to have achieved the same total wage. The high earning potential made working for CCS popular with drivers from a wide area but some could not stand the pace, or resist the temptation to collect a fare and not issue a ticket. This resulted in a high staff turnover, although a hard-core of 'old hands' found it suited them. Most drivers found the anti-social hours to be the worst aspect of the job, as the rolling rota worked backwards, invariably by one or two hours each day meaning that each duty started earlier than the previous day, not so much a problem on later shifts but difficult to adjust to on early starts, which was my weakness.

 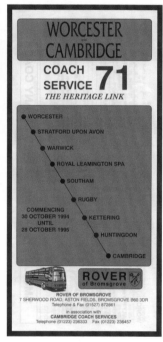

The Berkhof-bodied Volvo TXI 5497 seen previously on page 41 was a regular performer on service 71, seen here in Drummer Street about to depart for Worcester in 1995. **(Geoff Mills)**

The 'ROVER of Bromsgrove' logo incorporating the Bromsgrove Urban District Council coat of arms carried on coaches and timetables from 1995. **(Algar Signcraft)**

Following the departure of David Stevenson from the management of Rover Coaches, Ian Roberts announced in the August Staff Bulletin that from 29 July 1994 CCS would assume a degree of responsibility for Rover Coaches, although Rover would remain an autonomous subsidiary of Blazefield Holdings. With the change in management, the ROVER fleet name was re-designed in line with the CCS logo to incorporate the words 'ROVER of Bromsgrove', with the Bromsgrove Urban District Council coat of arms where the King`s College logo appeared on CCS vehicles. He also mentioned the demise of service 70, due to competition from both road and rail. There were plans for two new routes to commence on 30 October, one of which would cover part of the withdrawn service, with a stronger link to Rovers` base at Bromsgrove. Clever re-use of former PT route numbers led to the new service from Worcester to Cambridge being numbered 71, branded 'The Heritage Link'. This number had been used by PT for a summertime Saturday direct service from Worcester to Clacton-on-Sea, in the heyday of coach travel. The three daily return journeys would all be operated by Rover Coaches, following a cross country route via Stratford-upon-Avon, Warwick, Leamington Spa and Rugby, before joining the A14 to serve the previous stops on the service 70 timetable from Kettering to Cambridge.

On 30 October 1994 the stop on service 75 to serve the Imperial War Museum at Duxford was deleted and new service 74 was introduced. This followed an indirect route between Cambridge and Lowestoft on the East coast, calling at Newmarket, Mildenhall, Lakenheath, Brandon, Thetford, Attleborough, Wymondham, Norwich, Acle, Great Yarmouth and Gorleston before finally reaching Lowestoft 3 hours and 5 minutes later. NatEx had drastically reduced the frequency of their service 747 cross-country route which originated from the joint operation between Wessex, Percival`s of Oxford and PT which had previously been a two hourly service. Ian Roberts had already exploited part of this gap with the introduction of service 75 between Cambridge and Oxford and saw potential in the other direction east from Cambridge. There were four journeys each way at 0800, 1200, 1600 and 2000 from both Cambridge and Lowestoft. An outstation for one coach and three drivers was established at Lowestoft. As I was already familiar with most of the route, having driven the 747 for PT many times I went with another driver, Mick O`Nion to check out the stops in the Optimo midi-coach. We were scheduled to drive the route from Cambridge on the first day, passing new Lowestoft-based drivers Sid Hamilton and David Ward travelling in the opposite direction.

Bus stop sign and timetables were displayed at all stops on the new service to the usual high standards of Cambridge Coach Services as seen here at Mildenhall. **(David Slater)**

Driver Mick O`Nion pulls away from the bus stop in Wymondham at 0940 with F421 DUG, on the first service 74 journey bound for Lowestoft on 30 October 1994. **(Paul Hollingsbee)**

Driver Sid Hamilton pauses at Mildenhall on his first journey to Cambridge on service 74 on 30 October 1994 in F425 DUG. **(David Slater)**

CAMBRIDGE and LOWESTOFT
COACH SERVICE 74
THE EAST ANGLIA LINK

COMMENCING 30TH OCTOBER 1994 UNTIL 28TH OCTOBER 1995

GREAT YARMOUTH
NORWICH
WYMONDHAM
LOWESTOFT
ATTLEBOROUGH
THETFORD
LAKENHEATH
MILDENHALL
NEWMARKET
CAMBRIDGE

CAMBRIDGE
...a wealth of experience

CAMBRIDGE COACH SERVICES
KINGS HEDGES ROAD CAMBRIDGE CB4 4PQ ENGLAND
Telephone (01223) 236333   Fax (01223) 236457

The end of October may not have been the best time of year to start a service to the seaside, which meant that patronage on service 74 took time to build up, although there were several intermediate passengers in both directions. The F-reg 'low-drive' coaches were usually allocated, although the 18 seats in the Optimo were often sufficient. An exception being on 17 November, when I took it on the 1600 from Cambridge and had to phone for a larger coach, waiting at Marshalls on Newmarket Road for Paul Crocker, who had recently passed his PSV test to bring out coach number 367 for me to continue the journey.

The first pair of the eagerly-awaited new coaches arrived on 3 October, registered M301/2 BAV with matching fleet numbers, starting a new series which would eventually go as far as 325. The Plaxton Premiere 350 body with 52 reclining seats mounted on a Volvo B10M GL chassis would become the standard choice for the CCS fleet, although toilets were fitted to some later examples. The seats and interior panels were trimmed in grey/blue material to match the livery and incorporated several other detailed requirements to CCS specifications including pull down sun blinds and rubbish bins located just inside the door. These were larger than those specified by Wallace Arnold which had proved useful on the second-hand coaches in the fleet. A three-piece split windscreen was specified to accommodate the electronic destination display incorporating pantograph windscreen wipers. Brackets were fitted to accommodate Wayfarer ticket machines which could be removed when necessary.

On Christmas Day 1994 Chris Moody took the opportunity to line-up the eight new coaches in numerical order. On every other day of the year, the first one would have departed before the last one returned. **(Chris Moody)**

The interior of one of the new coaches shows the 52 seats upholstered to match the fleet colours. The driving seat, which could on some days be occupied for over 20 hours by up to six different drivers if engaged on three round trips to Gatwick or Oxford. **(Chris Moody)**

An example of 'what might have been'. Ian Roberts borrowed the number plate M100 CCS from Cambridge City Services, briefly applied to M301 BAV by Chris Moody, it was more likely to have been seen on the streets of Cambridge attached to a dustcart. **(Chris Moody)**

My first drive of 301 was on 8 October, taking over from Mark Neville at Gatwick to operate the 2200 journey service 79 to Cambridge. This was also the first time that I had driven an automatic coach, apart from collecting and returning Grey-Green coaches to Braintree after loan to CCS. 303-6 followed in November, 307/8 in December. The intention was that the eight new coaches should be used on the 78/9 airport services to maintain the modern image achieved but this was not always possible. On 14 December my rostered duty was 1600 service 74 to Lowestoft. As often happened, coaches were late returning from Gatwick resulting in my allocated coach being sent on the 1600 service 79, as the airport services were regarded as a priority. I went to Drummer Street in a van and took the next coach to come in, which happened to be 304. Even though I was late departing from Cambridge, I was able to enjoy driving a new coach to Lowestoft, take a 45 minute break and return on time.

As Cambridge Coach Services acquired no fewer than six coaches from the Wallace Arnold Tours fleet and hired several others, it is appropriate to include a photo of one of them in WA livery. The orange curtains and seat moquette were always a clue to their original owner. Fitting destination blinds and split windscreens added the CCS trademark, giving them an 'Expressliner' appearance. H647 UWR seen (left) in its youth and (right) prepared to meet its maker, showing SCARBOROUGH as a destination. (**Authors Collection /Chris Moody**)

On a cold and murky day, Paul Carter decided to visit Cambridge on 23 December 1994. His view of G95 RGG departing at 1300 for Oxford and G519 LWU engaged in a change of driver before returning to London on service 38 reminds the author of many similar days in Drummer Street. The muddy coaches and all-day use of headlights were a frequent experience for drivers. Paul also captured the arrival of the last of the new batch of coaches, M308 BAV. The dirty rear end of M304 BAV leaving the depot showing only lights and number plate washed indicates that the coach wash was out of use, probably frozen! (**Both Paul Carter**)

Grey-Green coaches continued in use at week-ends for several years with a Plaxton-bodied Volvo parked at Arbury Farm in June 1995. A month later a Duple Caribbean-bodied Volvo joins yet another hired former Wallace Arnold coach E305 UUB, on loan from Sovereign at Stevenage. (**Both David Beardmore**)

Four of the five E-reg coaches transferred to Bromsgrove in their various guises. 363 with the new fleet name in Worcester, en-route to Cambridge on service 71 on 21 July 1995. **(David Cole)** *359 parked at Cambridge after withdrawl, with fleet names removed awaiting disposal in February 1996.* **(Richard Haughey)** *362 in wintry surroundings engaged on local service 872 to Wolverley High School on 2 March 1995 and 360 carrying the old-style 'ROVER' logo in Redditch on route 177 to* KINGS HEATH *on 14 January 1995.* **(Both David Cole)**

The arrival of the new coaches allowed 361-3 to join 359/60 with Rover Coaches, 365/6 went north to East Yorkshire, and 367 to Keighley & District. The requirement for eight new coaches was not a random number to order, but a theoretical allocation to cover the airport services. The first one going out on the 0200 to Gatwick, returning at 0600 as the first departure from Gatwick, followed on the next seven hourly departures of the rest of the batch. With the first coach due back in Cambridge at 0900, it could be scheduled for a second trip at 1000, with the other seven coaches following at hourly intervals until 1700. By then the first coach should have returned from its second journey in time to operate a third journey at 1800, followed by the next two coaches on the 1900 and final 2000 journeys. This schedule could involve three coaches doing three round trips in 21 hours, if returning late they were unable to return to the depot to be re-fuelled during the day. On several occasions a coach has been known to run out of fuel returning to Cambridge on the third journey, in my experience once in Regent Street, almost in sight of Drummer Street and even closer to home a coach spluttered to a stop in Arbury Road, yards from the depot.

Like many of Ian Roberts' carefully planned operations, things looked better on paper than in reality. Very heavy traffic, particularly on the M25 motorway resulted in long delays in coaches returning to Cambridge. The strain on traffic office staff, who worked 12 hour shifts was enormous. Andy Gibbs had a novel way of relieving his stress. The daily running sheets were always written in pencil, to facilitate last minute changes by rubbing out and changing drivers names and coach numbers. When under pressure, he would snap a pencil in half and throw it out of the window. When reporting for a late shift, I could tell how the day had been by the size of the pile of broken pencils beneath the office window. He would often say "Go to Kilmaine Close and 'steal' a coach from Premier, or else wait in Drummer Street for a coach to come in". Stealing a coach from Premier was a regular occurrence, but was sometimes reciprocated to mutual benefit.

On one such occasion I was sent to 'borrow' a Premier coach for the 1800 Gatwick service that had already been prepared to depart on a tour early the next morning. I had strict instructions on my return to make sure it was refuelled and clean before taking it to the Viscount depot at Peterborough, where some Premier coaches were based at the time. On arrival at Peterborough, I found the gates locked, so had to return the coach to Kilmaine Close, presumably resulting in a late departure for the tour a few hours later.

In March 1995 Andy Gibbs left to join Biss Bros Coaches at Bishops Stortford as General Manager, resulting in the appointment of Roger Birch to Operations Manager and Paul Crocker as his assistant. Additional journeys introduced on 9 April to service 75 at 0300 and 1100, returning from Oxford at 0700 and 1500 boosted the increasingly popular service to eight journeys in each direction every day. An additional service 78 journey via Luton Airport at 1900 increased the number from eight to nine but the last service 78 departure from Gatwick changed from 2400 to 2300 to maintain the alternating hourly variations between the Stansted and Luton routes. In an attempt to improve reliability in departures from Heathrow in the morning peak, a new duty was created by sending an empty coach from Cambridge from Monday to Friday to operate a 0845 relief from Terminal Four, as the 0800 service 79 from Gatwick was invariably late due to the heavy commuter traffic on the M25 motorway.

This increase in work resulted in the driving rota rising from 42 to 49 lines. With an incredibly comprehensive Day and Holiday Tour programme usually covered by the second-hand Paramount 3500 coaches, vehicle allocation was always tight. The late cancellation of a tour enabled one of the new coaches, M307 BAV to be entered into the British Coach Rally at Brighton on 22/23 April. Driven by Martin Carr, with Martin Shaw as navigator they both put in great efforts to present the coach in pristine condition, despite the 107,000 kilometres accumulated in just four months service. This was to be the only time that a CCS coach entered the rally, although D350 KVE had been entered at Brighton when new (page 16), also joining Expressliner G382 REG at Southampton in 1990 while Premier was under AJS Group ownership.

Four consecutively numbered M-reg coaches seen in geographic locational order. North to South: 304 at Cambridge Drummer Street, 305 at Heathrow Central Bus Station, 306 in the coach park at Gatwick Airport and 307 on Madeira Drive in Brighton, while taking part in the British Coach Rally in April 1995. **(304/307 Trevor Brookes, 305 Author`s Collection, 306 Alan Conway)**

Contrasting weather in March 1995 as H647 UWR approaches Mildenhall (left) on its way to Lowestoft on the 0800 service 74 from Cambridge. Nine days later on 12 March, G95 RGG (right) passes Wymondham Police Station (now demolished) in glorious sunshine, heading for Cambridge. **(David Slater/Paul Hollingsbee)**

Extensive marketing to promote service 74 saw the route diverted between Gorleston and Lowestoft to serve Pleasurewood Hills, a popular theme park throughout the summer season. Special inclusive tickets were available in advance, combining the admission and coach fare. This service was well patronised, particularly by day trippers to Great Yarmouth, often requiring relief coaches at weekends. With a favourable weather forecast, a second coach would often be sent from Cambridge. This could also be supplemented if needed by another coach provided by Semmence Coaches from Wymondham, strategically based between Thetford and Norwich, where overloads were most likely to occur.

An arrangement was made with Paul Hollingsbee, Claims Director of Blazefield Group Insurance, whose office was located in Norwich. Paul lived in Wymondham and drove part-time for Semmence, so was available to stand-by on Saturdays and Sundays. Semmence would make a coach available and Paul would await a phone call from the CCS base. They were in touch with the service 74 driver who indicated where a relief would be needed from, usually at Thetford, but sometimes Brandon or Mildenhall. Relief coaches were not often required beyond Great Yarmouth, where they parked-up for the day until the peak return journey.

This system worked well for three summers, until the arrival in 1998 of the double-deckers, reducing the need for reliefs. Only once was a relief required in the opposite direction. One Saturday in July 1997 soon after Paul had received a call to say he was not needed to go to Great Yarmouth, a second call came to say that the coach from Lowestoft had just picked up 30 passengers in Great Yarmouth. They had purchased day returns to Cambridge, could he provide a relief from Norwich to Cambridge, returning at 1700?

Semmence provided relief coaches on busy summer weekends for service 74, driven by Paul Hollingsbee. Plaxton-bodied Dennis Javelin RJI 5721 is seen at the bus stop outside the old Norfolk and Norwich Hospital (left) on Sunday 6 August 1995 following H647 UWR and (right), two weeks later a DAF at the Market Gates in Great Yarmouth with Jim Woodburn about to continue through to Lowestoft with his regular coach D350 KVE. Another Jim, (the author) would take-over on return to Cambridge to drive the 1600 and 2000 return service 74 journeys with the same coach that day. **(Both Paul Hollingsbee)**

Service 38 was also diverted to serve Audley End House, near Saffron Walden at weekends. Other opportunities for day trips were advertised by special 'fliers' indicating how passengers could enjoy days out by using existing services, often with a choice of return times. To help with the increase in work, G62 RGG was transferred within Blazefield from Northern Rose, whose livery it retained for a while. New to Parks of Hamilton, it was from the same batch as G95-8 RGG, so fitted into the fleet well.

In an attempt to boost the seasonal Saturday summer holiday service 72 to Bournemouth, it was extended to Weymouth from 27 May 1995. 'Go as you please' holidays were offered in conjunction with local hotels in Bournemouth, Weymouth, Guernsey and Jersey, utilising the coach service and Condor Catamaran service from Weymouth to the Channel Isles. This proved to be the final year of operation of this route, leading to another link with the original Premier Travel Group ending on 30 September. These holidays were just four pages in a 50 page colour coach holiday brochure published that year, offering a huge selection of Classic Day Tours, extended day tours involving overnight travel, UK and continental coach breaks and holidays.

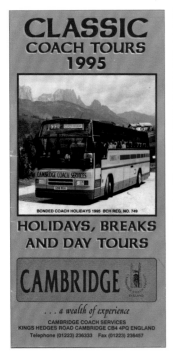

Homeward bound from the Mildenhall Air Fete on 28 May 1995, the Van Hool-bodied Volvo YXI 2747 also shown on page 35 as B490 UNB now sports the 'ROVER of Bromsgrove' name across the front, although the 'ROVER COACHES' logo is still apparent on the side. The recently opened A14 link road would have speeded the passengers (who had each paid a £13 fare inclusive of admission) on their way. **(Trevor Brookes)**

The colour cover of the 50 page 1995 Cambridge Coach Tours brochure contrasts with the 1995 Classic Coach Tours leaflet produced in timetable format for Rover of Bromsgrove, listing a comprehensive selection of day trips from May to September, including a 90 minute pick-up schedule throughout much of the West Midlands.

Showing service 69 WEYMOUTH on the destination, E359 NEG is about to depart from Bromsgrove on 22 July 1995 on a route also mentioned in the above leaflet, serving Weston-Super-Mare en-route to Weymouth. Advertised to run on Saturdays and Sundays from 27 May - 10 September and daily in school holidays (July/August) with a return fare of £11 (half-fare for Senior Citizens and Children) **(David Cole)**

In a surprising move, the Associated Bus & Coach Investments Ltd licence was surrendered in May 1995. A new licence was granted in the West Midlands traffic area to Cambridge Coach Services Limited for two double-deck and 16 single-deck vehicles, although they were not all needed, as many vehicles had already been disposed of. At this point the Rover of Bromsgrove fleet was believed to consist of eight coaches, only three of which had originated with Rover, the other five comprising of E359-63 NEG from the parent fleet.

Anticipating competition, a ninth daily journey from Cambridge to Oxford at 1900, returning at 2300 was introduced on 10 September. A serious threat to the viability of service 75 arose when Stagecoach United Counties commenced a new hourly cross-country service between Cambridge and Oxford, numbered X5 on 25 September 1995. Although only the termini at Drummer Street and Gloucester Green were common to both services, the introductory fares between the University cities were low. CCS had only increased the original fare between Cambridge and Oxford from £11 to £12 single in April but were forced to reduce it to £7 from the 30 October, with no chance to increase it again for several years. This had a knock-on effect on revenue, as the fare from Oxford to Stansted Airport had been the same as that to Cambridge since the inception of the service, so also had to be reduced in line.

The Inter-Varsity 'Crossed Oars' symbol applied to coaches on the Oxford service did not last long. Fortunately Chris Moody posed G97 RGG for these shots thus adorned before they entered service. **(All Chris Moody)**

In an attempt to promote a superior service, Ian Roberts decided that only coaches with toilets would operate service 75. With the seasonal reduction in tours and day trips the G-reg coaches would be allocated to the Oxford run. At least G96/7 RGG were adorned with vinyl 'crossed oars' in light and dark blue University colours on the rear window and lower panels behind the front wheels. Large white lettering listing CAMBRIDGE – STANSTED AIRPORT – AMERSHAM – HIGH WYCOMBE – OXFORD applied to the top of side windows completed the route branding. Many will agree that route branding only works when the vehicle is engaged exclusively on the promoted route, this was not always possible due to the intensive nature of the CCS operation. Fellow Directors also failed to share Ian`s enthusiasm for the 'crossed oars' and they were soon peeled off.

As well as expressing concern about the competition and urging drivers to make every effort to retain custom, the September Staff Bulletin also announced an order had been placed for four more new coaches. They would be built to the same specification as the initial eight but fitted with toilets. In theory, they could have operated the 75 service by the first coach doing three round trips with a 60 minute turnaround at each end and the other three on two trips each. A change in policy saw them enter service the following February to the same specification as the previous eight coaches with 52 seats and no toilets.

As short term tenants at Arbury Farm, an eye had been kept out for suitable premises to establish a new depot, leading to a planning application during the summer to convert the former yard of Marlows the builders merchants at Nuffield Road into a coach depot. Approval was granted in October, with the optimistic hope of occupancy some time the next spring. Although there was no longer a link in ownership with Premier Travel Agency, a good relationship was maintained. The chain acted as booking agents for CCS daytrips, tours and express services. An arrangement also existed

for Premier customers who booked their holidays and took out Premier's own travel insurance to receive free tickets to the airport on CCS services. Such co-operation also included complimentary coach travel to agency staff and discount on holidays booked by CCS staff with Premier agencies.

When Drummer Street bus station was rebuilt in 1986, all long distance coaches were allocated to bays 12 – 15, outside the bus station. At certain times four bays were insufficient to accommodate all the arriving and departing vehicles, especially when relief coaches were needed. The introduction of the Stagecoach X5 service to Oxford with hourly departures in September 1995 made the situation worse. From 29 October 1995 agreement was reached with NatEx for CCS to provide a Controller to cover a one third share of supervision over both companies' services at Drummer Street. To ease congestion CCS service 38 departures to London were moved to bay seven in the bus station. Service 74 to Lowestoft was also moved into the bus station on bay five and the times changed to an hour later from both ends on all departures at 0900, 1300, 1700 and 2100.

Special airport services timetables were issued every year for distribution from Premier Travel Agencies advertising the free facility offered to customers. **(Both David Slater)**

As mentioned above the London service 38 departures were moved to inside the bus station from October 1995. The author is at the wheel of G97 RGG leaving Drummer Street at 1300 on 9 April 1996.
(Trevor Brookes)

F885 RFP was registered YXI 2749 from 3/93-3/96 as seen on page 41. Joining the parent fleet on the demise of Rover early in 1996, it soon became CCS 385 with original registration as can be seen leaving High Wycombe bus station (right) in September that year returning from Oxford, driven by the author. **(M.A.Penn)**

Another change with the introduction of winter timetables saw a fourth journey added to service 71. All journeys were extended from Worcester to Bromsgrove, with an additional stop in Droitwich. Another additional stop between Huntingdon and Cambridge was established at Papworth Hospital, taking the total running time to four hours. New departure times were 0400, 0800, 1200 and 1600 from Bromsgrove, returning from Cambridge at 0900, 1300, 1700 and 2100. The early and late journeys removed the need for a driver to sleep-out in Cambridge. In line with current trends, a limited service of four journeys, four hours apart was introduced on service 79 between Cambridge, Stansted, Heathrow and Gatwick on Boxing Day.

G62 RGG the fifth RGG-reg coach arrived in May 1995 in Northern Rose livery (left) initially on hire to Cambridge Coach Services. It was eventually repainted and joined the fleet and seen (right) in Kettering bus station heading for Bromsgrove on service 71 on 1 June 1996. **(Chris Moody/David Beardmore)**

When Stagecoach took over CHL in January 1996, their NatEx and other coaching activities were moved to the main Cambus depot at Cowley Road. The Kilmaine Close premises were no longer an operational base by the end of the month. In February the Rover of Bromsgrove subsidiary ceased to exist after the termination of most local authority contracts. To operate the long standing staff contract for the Frankley M5 Motorway Service Area and the established service 71 between Bromsgrove and Cambridge, a CCS outstation was established at Bromsgrove with a requirement for three coaches and six drivers. The three coaches initially based at Bromsgrove carrying CCS logos were 360/1 and 349, which briefly carried its Rover inspired select registration YXI 2749 before reverting to the original F885 RFP mark with new fleet number 385 in March. The remaining Rover coaches were disposed of and subsequently any coach that was available made its way to Bromsgrove on service 71.

As mentioned above the 71 service from Bromsgrove became a Cambridge Coach Services operation in February 1996. Former Rover drivers joined the CCS team to drive most journeys, although it was sometimes necessary to send a driver from Cambridge in latter days. Various coaches can be seen here leaving Huntingdon bus station.
(All M.A. Penn)

Rear view of N311/2 VAV (left) newly delivered in February 1996 and front of 312 (right) before destination blinds and rear wheel trims have been fitted. **(David Beardmore/Richard Haughey)**

The arrival in February 1996 of four more new coaches, registered N309-12 VAV enabled five older coaches to go to Sovereign at Stevenage to fill a gap in Green Line requirements. 321/4/5/58/62 were all repainted in Green Line livery to operate the service 797 between London Victoria and Cambridge taken over from The Shires on 17 March. Sovereign had ordered three new coaches for the contract but delivery was not expected until the end of the year. Total repaints of inter-group transfers were rare, but when the three new Green Line coaches arrived at Stevenage in December, F421/4 DUG were returned to Cambridge and repainted in full CCS livery. F425 DUG remained at Stevenage as a spare coach, while E358/62 NEG were sold. Another unusual instance of repainting had occurred in October 1994, when F884 RFP, by then renumbered 384 went north to join the Northern Rose fleet, receiving their livery. The following May similar coach G62 RGG came south in Northern Rose livery, but was soon repainted in CCS style grey/blue as seen on page 53.

*Resplendent in Green Line livery, with bold blue '**SOVEREIGN**' names F425 DUG (left) pauses in Stevenage bus station on the way to Cambridge, while sister F424 DUG (right) has lost her '797' route branding when seen entering Luton bus station heading for Stevenage from Gatwick on Jetlink 747 duties in 1996.* **(Both M.A.Penn)**

Departing from Cambridge bus station on Green Line 797 service (left), the larger area of yellow at the front of E358 NEG emphasises the difference between standard and 'low-drive' Paramount 3200 bodies. F421 DUG is seen (right) back at Cambridge before repaint into standard grey/blue for further use as seen on pages 53 and 62. **(David Beardmore/Chris Moody)**

A new airport service branded the Suffolk-Essex Airport Link commenced on 17 March 1996. Ian Roberts had explored the possibility of a service from Ipswich to Heathrow, via Stansted. His original plan was for a route following part of the former joint Eastern Counties/Premier Travel 'Eastline' 792 service between Ipswich and Newmarket, calling at Stowmarket and Bury St Edmunds and had reconnoitred the route by car with drivers rep Brian Camps. No doubt AirLinks would not have taken kindly to a stop in Newmarket, as they served the town with their Jetlink 747 service from Norwich to the airports. The coaching arm of municipally-owned Ipswich Buses had experimented with a service to Stansted Airport in 1990, using a 19-seat midi-bus which failed to attract much support. As with any airport service, regular journeys throughout the day and night were needed to attract regular custom.

Service 76 ran between Ipswich and Heathrow Airport. N312 VAV is seen here (left) about to depart from The Old Cattle Market bus station in Ipswich. At the opposite end of the route M307 BAV can be seen in the West Ramp coach park at Heathrow (right) on 22 October 1996 after operating the 1000 journey from Ipswich. **(Chris Moody/Author)**

Service 76 started with six journeys each way, coaches leaving Ipswich and Heathrow every four hours from 0200 to 2200 with a running time of 2 hours 50 minutes. Bus stations at Colchester, Braintree and Stansted Airport were served, along with several intermediate stops. Connections to Gatwick from Heathrow, and Oxford and Cambridge from Stansted were advertised. In theory the service could be operated by two coaches, usually from the newest batch by running light between Cambridge and Stansted. Through passengers would change there, the coach returning to Cambridge to refuel and change driver. After three round trips, the fuel gauge would be showing low, sometimes giving concern for the last few miles along the M11 motorway. During the day crew changes would be achieved by a service 76 driver travelling as passenger to Stansted on a service 79 coach, the relieved driver returning to Cambridge by the same method. This procedure added a couple of hours to the duty, which made it a good earner for drivers.

Former Green Line Leyland Tiger B264 KPF, now painted white with blue '**SOVEREIGN**' lettering was on loan again in March and used on Airport services. A tachograph-equipped 12-seat Ford Transit minibus joined the fleet in full fleet livery for crew changes and route learning expeditions. Good news for drivers in April was the completion of a bus lane on Milton Road, which made it easier to travel from the depot to Drummer Street. Not so good news was the introduction of a ban on coaches and lorries using the third lane of motorways for a two year trial period, we all now know that it became permanent, with little consultation!

Small vehicles in the fleet were all Fords, ranging from this 12 seat PSV licensed Transit minibus (left) to the Tourneo and Escort vans (right) used by the engineers and inspectors. **(Trevor Brookes/Chris Moody)**

In May Stagecoach reduced the Premier Travel Services (PTS) commitment to NatEx diagrams, causing Ian Roberts to deny rumours that CCS had plans to take on any of this work. Several former Wallace Arnold Volvo coaches painted plain white were hired at various times to cover for accident repairs to F885 RFP, and warranty work on the four N-reg coaches. There was a pair of H-reg Paramount 3500s, which at times carried the magnetic CCS fleet name and logo which could be attached to unliveried coaches and J749 CWT with an early Plaxton Premiere 350 body, on which a full 'Cambridge Coach Services' fleet name was applied to the front panel. This coach may later have been acquired by Sovereign, as it was also seen with blue 'SOVEREIGN' names while still painted white, eventually receiving full Green Line 797 livery while at Stevenage.

The newest of the hired coaches was J749 CWT (left). A ticket machine was fitted and the blue fleet name applied to the front. The magnetic logo on the side was easily moved from one coach to another as can be seen on H658 UWR (right), to which destination equipment had been fitted by a previous hirer, enabling route number 71 to be displayed as it approaches Drummer Street from Bromsgrove on 5 November 1996. **(Chris Moody/Trevor Brookes)**

In the spring of 1996 the diesel tank at Arbury Farm became unfit for use, due to the constant effects of water from the coach wash. A new portable tank with integrated bund arrived and can be seen here being unloaded by crane. A year later the crane would return to transfer the tank to Kilmaine Close. **(Chris Moody)**

Timetable changes introduced on 27 October saw the 0400 from Bromsgrove and 2100 from Cambridge service 71 journeys withdrawn, reintroducing a sleep-out for Bromsgrove-based drivers in Cambridge. The vehicle allocation and staff numbers at Lowestoft outstation were doubled to provide total cover for service 74, depriving Cambridge-based drivers of a change of scenery, the monotony of motorway driving and a whiff of sea air. An early morning journey from Lowestoft at 0500 proved popular with commuters into Cambridge and the poorly patronised final journey at 2100 from Lowestoft to Cambridge was withdrawn.

The recently introduced service 76 had the last and first journeys between Stansted and Heathrow removed, still leaving six return journeys between Ipswich and Stansted. The stop at Coggeshall was replaced by a new stop at Witham, resulting in a slight detour. Another innovation was the listing in the service 78/79 timetable from March to October of service 76 journeys from Heathrow to Cambridge at 0200 and 0600, utilising a vehicle change-over and previous light running between Cambridge and Stansted. These manoeuvres also enabled a 0100 and 2200 departure from Cambridge to Stansted, which combined with the bi-hourly Oxford 75 service increased the number of daily journeys available from 19 to 21. Even if no passengers were carried fuel tax rebate could be claimed on a registered service.

The pair of new coaches which proved more suitable for private hire can be seen here fitted with white disposable headrest covers, P313 CVE (left) and P314 CVE (right). **(Ken Worland/Chris Moody)**

By November 1996 the former PTS depot at Kilmaine Close was being used to store withdrawn Cambus vehicles. When it was put up for sale the management of CCS showed an interest, as there had been complications with the proposed premises at Nuffield Road. Kilmaine Close would be far more suitable and was already established as a coach depot. The opportunity to acquire a pair of new coaches built to Expressliner specifications was taken in December. The chassis and body numbers of P313/4 CVE were lower than those of N309-12 VAV which had been delivered in February, indicating that they could have been built the previous year. The livery and interior trim was finished to the usual CCS specification but the lack of a rear window and fitting of continental style rear emergency door made them stand out from the rest of the fleet. They were also the first new coaches to be fitted with a toilet and lap seat belts on all seats, the latter feature making them popular on school outings with safety conscious parents at a time when these were not widely fitted on coaches. The new arrivals enabled 360/1 to be withdrawn, the last of the E-reg batch that had given such good service, although 350/1, the last two D-reg Van Hools remained in service.

Until then the Paramount 3500-bodied coaches were still the usual choice for tours and private hire but were all showing signs of age, as they were also used intensively on express services between other duties. From a passenger`s point of view the older coaches were more comfortable and gave better all-round vision, as the first few rows of seats sloped

Passing through Great Yarmouth on service 74 in August 1996 (left) E361 NEG is once again a Cambridge coach after service with Rover at Bromsgrove. 360/1 stayed together throughout their careers, being transferred to Rover where they served with others of the same batch. After further use at Cambridge, they were replaced by the new coaches 313/4, seen ready for disposal (right) in December 1996. They stayed together, joining 362 at Hearn`s Coaches, Harrow Weald who re-registered the trio NIL 9246-8 in October 1997. **(M.A.Penn/Chris Moody)**

CLASSIC DAY TOURS

The G-reg Paramount 3500 coaches were regular performers on coach hire and tours until 1996, some of which are posed here for publicity shots. **(All Chris Moody)**

towards the front in 'theatre' style. The destination boxes did not take up the whole of the top windscreen, giving better forward vision. The Premiere 350 body was more 'box-shaped', with all seats mounted at the same level, high above the driver. As the destination equipment occupied the whole of the top windscreen, forward vision was limited, even to front seat passengers. However the facility of an on-board toilet made 313/4 popular for long journeys, particularly the extended day tours to places such as Amsterdam, Brugge, Dublin, Edinburgh and Paris Disneyland which all involved overnight travel.

DAYS OUT BY COACH

DAILY FROM CAMBRIDGE

CAMBRIDGE

...a wealth of experience

Ready to depart on a private hire when new in February 1996 is N310 VAV. **(David Beardmore)**

First appearing on the cover of the summer 1997 day trip leaflet, M303 BAV was posed in front of Audley End House, with Simon Matthews at the wheel.

One of the extended Classic Day Tours was to Edinburgh. Departing from Cambridge at midnight and arriving on Waverley Bridge in the Scottish Capital at 0730, where P313 CVE is seen on 2 August 1997. Passengers then had the opportunity to stretch their legs before re-joining the coach for a 90 minute city tour accompanied by a blue badge guide.

*A stop was made at the Palace of Holyroodhouse, where the coach can be seen awaiting returning passengers. The weary driver then enjoyed a hotel room for the day while passengers made the most of their free time before gathering on Waverley Bridge at 1800 to board the coach for their return journey. The fare of £20 was good value for the distance travelled and up to 30 hours away from home. **(All David Slater)***

Chapter 4 BIG CHANGES - ANOTHER MOVE

On the occasion of what proved to be the last staff dinner to be held at King`s College on 11 January 1997, Ian Roberts proudly announced that negotiations were proceeding to acquire the former Premier Travel (PT) premises at Kilmaine Close. Confirmation of the purchase was given in the Staff Bulletin dated 26 February. A considerable amount of work was required to re-equip the premises, including installing a coach wash and moving the large diesel tank from Kings Hedges Road. Most of the concrete around the buildings had to be broken up and re-laid, as well as extensive refurbishment of the offices and workshop. The anticipated date of completion at the end of May proved to be optimistic, before finally moving in on 28 June.

The delay could have been caused by the sudden death of Ian Roberts, from a major heart attack on 29 April. After spending so much time and effort seeking suitable premises to accommodate 'his' coach company, it seemed so unfair that he should not live to see his work come to fruition. At least he was aware of his success, even if he did not see the company name in large letters across the front of the workshop where the name 'Premier Travel' had once been displayed. Although nobody guessed at the time, the 'Cambridge Coach Services' (CCS) name would only last for a few years, to be replaced by 'AirLinks' and subsequently 'National Express' (NatEx), as can be seen in photos on pages 81/4 and 88/9. Within ten years the premises would be demolished.

Certain members of staff considered Ian to be slightly eccentric, some of his ideas seemed over optimistic but some proved to be fruitful. He made a point of taking a turn as weekend controller, sometimes a daunting 12 hour shift. Dressed for the part in white shirt, black uniform tie and epaulettes, his face would greet all drivers clocking on through the hatch between the traffic office and driver`s lockers. He was usually accompanied by his dogs 'Whisky' and 'Soda' and a spare driver`s duties could include taking them 'walkies' in the yard. Ian enjoyed these opportunities to chat with drivers, sometimes receiving useful feedback. Answering the telephone also enlightened him to matters that might not have otherwise come to his attention. His many contacts proved invaluable in times of crisis, sometimes surprising even himself! His favourite words when a task was accomplished, were 'splendid' or 'marvellous'. The smile on his face confirmed his satisfaction.

He had a habit of blending in amongst the crowds, often travelling to meetings by coach where his casual boarding could surprise the driver. Regular meetings with BAA officials at Heathrow Airport kept him in personal contact with activities at Central Bus Station. One Sunday I arrived at Gloucester Green in Oxford, having just driven the 0500 service 75 from Cambridge. Ian was standing there with a broad smile on his face, hiding his disappointment at the lack of passengers on my coach. "You made an early start this morning" I said, "not really", he replied, "I am on my way home from the Black & White staff reunion at Cheltenham".

This is how many people remember Ian Roberts, with a smile on his face and a bottle in his hand as he celebrates an award to his company. **(Roger Birch Collection)**

Ian was well known and respected throughout the industry, and always found time for enthusiasts, as he had been one himself, photographing PT vehicles as a teenager. His funeral was held at Cambridge Crematorium on 7 May 1997, attended by over 200 people, proof of his popularity if it were needed. I did not attend, as I was driving coach 314 on the 1500 service 78 from Gatwick that day. As I passed through Hunton Bridge on time at 1630, I noticed a funeral taking place at Langleybury Church. That was the only time I ever saw a funeral there in all the hundreds of times that I have passed through, what a strange coincidence I thought to myself. I have often said to former CCS colleagues that it was better that Ian was cremated and not buried, as he would have turned in his grave if he could have seen some of the subsequent happenings at Kilmaine Close!

In his honour, the newly re-furbished building was named 'ROBERTS HOUSE', marked by a suitably inscribed plaque adjacent to the foundation stone laid by Messrs Lainson and Matthews in 1976. Another tribute to Ian was to name the newest coach in the fleet 'Ian Roberts', in blue vinyl letters above both front wheels, below his inspired company logo. An engraved brass plate inside the coach informed passengers of the significance. As a modest person, Ian might have felt embarrassed, also I am sure that he would have thought it to be a 'splendid' tribute.

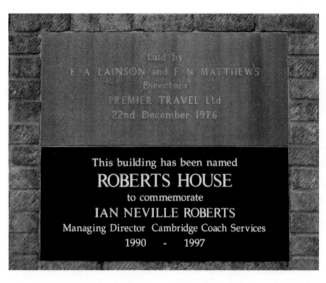

The stone plaque to commemorate Ian Roberts contribution to Cambridge Coach Services set into the wall at Kilmaine Close. **(Paul Carter)**

Newly delivered coach on 17 March 1997 before destination blind and number plates were fitted. **(Ken Worland)**

The sudden loss of Ian caused some changes to management. Roger Birch continued in his role as Operations Manager with the added responsibility of day to day supervision of CCS. He would report to David Hurry, who would split his time between the two Blazefield companies at Stevenage and Cambridge in his new role as Blazefield Group Operations Director South. The new coach mentioned above was registered P315 DVE, the usual Volvo/Plaxton 52 seat combination, with no toilet. This addition enabled the sale of D351 KVE, leaving disabled coach D350 KVE as the last of the original Van Hools in the fleet.

The new coach was registered P315 DVE and regarded as the flagship of the fleet, being named after Ian Roberts instead of a Cambridge College. On 13 June 1998 the same coach is seen here at the Channel Tunnel UK terminal while engaged on a day trip to Brussels. **(Both David Slater)**

D350 KVE was the longest serving coach in the fleet, remaining until March 1999. Sister 351 also out-lived some of the newer coaches, being replaced by 315 two years earlier. **(Paul Carter/Chris Moody)**

Roberts House was the first freehold premises in the Blazefield Group, the two story office block providing more spacious accommodation than the Portakabins previously occupied. A training room was established in what had originally been the PT board room. Apart from instruction in the use of Wayfarers and other basic procedures, tachograph legislation was also explained to new drivers. Mac Law was appointed as Company Training Officer. Although he had recently retired from a career in the Police force, he came from a family with strong PT roots, his father Harry had been a senior driver, his mother a conductress and an aunt and two uncles were also long serving employees. Mac had driven coaches part-time for both Kenzie's and CCS, more recently qualifying as a Driving Instructor with East Anglian Driver Training.

Jim Woodburn gives an elderly customer easy access to his coach on a private hire. **(Frank Bird Photography)**

In addition to training unqualified drivers to enable them to obtain a PCV entitlement to their licence, the Training Officer also took steps to raise the standards of existing drivers. From time to time a supplement to the Staff Bulletin was issued entitled 'Coachcraft', giving advice and information to drivers. An opportunity was also provided for any driver who wished to receive additional training in their own time, leading to a test with the Institute of Advanced Motorists. Several drivers were successful in obtaining the coveted certificate and badge.

In the autumn the vacated former premises at Arbury Farm were advertised to rent at £20K per annum. Soon after travellers moved onto the site again, but I doubt if they paid any rent! Several years would pass before the site was re-developed, in the meantime part was leased as a second-hand car sales area.

Minor changes to the service 75 timetable commencing 26 October saw the addition of a stop at Piddington on the A40 between West Wycombe and Stokenchurch. For the first time, four return journeys between Cambridge and Oxford at four

Passing through Great Yarmouth on 28 August 1997, F421 DUG looks smart in the second application of Cambridge Coach Services' livery after spending time as a Green Line coach at Stevenage as seen on Page 54. **(M.A.Penn)**

hourly intervals were run on Boxing Day, 26 December, operated by two coaches. The timings arranged to slot in between the six service 79 journeys to give an enhanced frequency between Cambridge and Stansted Airport on that day.

More bad news for drivers in January 1998 was that new legislation regarding speed limiters fitted to coaches meant that vehicles used on international journeys had to be restricted to 100 kph (62.4 mph) by 1 July 1998. Those operating in the UK had a further year to comply but due to the varied nature of work undertaken, the Engineering Director decreed that all coaches in the fleet would be dealt with as they became due for calibration. This reduction in top speed and the experimental third lane ban imposed in May 1996, which looked set to become permanent made the three hour running time on most services impossible to achieve, unless traffic conditions were light, which was rare.

Annual wage negotiations had previously been agreed between management and elected drivers representatives, the commission element being related to ticket sales on the coach. Hourly rates had risen from £4.20 in 1995, to £4.35 in 1996. The loss of Ian Roberts had changed the relationship between management and some drivers, with management keen to abolish commission. When an aspiration to move toward an hourly rate of £6 for drivers was indicated, the swift reply was that this was not immediately achievable. Figures were produced to show that the average commission between November 1996 and October 1997 equated to 93.53 pence per hour. Various combinations of split commission and lower rates for part-time and new employees were explored, with a maximum consolidated rate of £4.90 being offered. Negotiations dragged on throughout November and December, resulting in a final offer being imposed in January 1998 of £5.62 per hour for full-time drivers, but lower rates for part-time and new starters. Typically duty times were reduced to give an element of productivity, so the net pay hours were also reduced.

New timetables commencing on 29 March reflected the lower permitted speed, with most daytime journeys on service 75 increased by up to 15 minutes. Service 78/79 journey times were increased by up to 20 minutes between Gatwick and Heathrow, allowing for delays on the M25 motorway and give more realistic departure times from Heathrow. The opportunity to redesign timetable leaflets was taken at this date, as most of the services except 38 were changed, some drastically. The new leaflets had more pages but still folded down to the same size to fit in publicity racks. They were brighter and bolder than the old timetables, the style of which dated back to PT days. A colour photo of one of the latest coaches was printed on the cover, each doctored to show the appropriate destination display for that service. Another useful feature was location maps of principal stops.

Former Wallace Arnold coach H647 UWR calls at the recently opened Riverside Bus Station at Stratford-upon-Avon, heading for Cambridge on service 71 on 25 April 1998. **(David Beardmore)**

Service 71 times were changed slightly and only the first eastbound and last return journeys served Bromsgrove and Droitwich. Crew changes at Worcester during the day enabled three return journeys between Worcester and Cambridge to continue. Two extra stops were introduced in Godmanchester and the stop in Stratford-upon-Avon was moved from Bridge Street to the new Riverside Bus Station.

Service 74 changes saw the closure of Lowestoft outstation. With the exception of Roy Edmonds, drivers were made redundant. He had experience in driver training and transferred to Cambridge to assist Mac Law in the increasingly busy driving school. There were still four return journeys between Cambridge and Norwich at 0630, 0830, 1330 and 1730 but only the 0830 and 1330 departures would continue to Great Yarmouth and Lowestoft. An additional journey from Thetford at 0645 to Cambridge to cater for commuters entailed a coach running light from Cambridge. The stop in Great Yarmouth was moved from the Market Gates to the Market Place. A detour was added to serve the main gate of RAF Lakenheath and the stop at Marshall`s on Newmarket Road in Cambridge was moved closer to the City at Ivett and Reed`s.

Service 76 also saw drastic changes from six evenly-spaced journeys throughout 24 hours to nine journeys which operated every two hours during peak periods. There were also some short workings between Ipswich and Stansted early morning and late at night requiring a third coach to provide the increased service. The stop at Witham was replaced by one at Bradwell, shortening the journey between Braintree and Marks Tey by ten minutes. A new stop was established at London Colney, just off junction 22 of the M25 motorway adjacent to Sainsbury`s Savacentre, also served by local buses giving connections to St Albans. The service 75 also called there, but not the 79.

Volvo Olympian R91 GTM had departed from Cambridge at 0630 on a daily short working to Norwich when caught by David Slater in Mildenhall at 0710 on 19 June 1998. **(David Slater)**

Service 78 introduced an additional short working from Cambridge at 0600 to Luton Airport, returning at 0715. This gave an earlier northbound journey than previously available. Special family tickets were offered on all routes except service 38, marketed as 'Family Fives'. They cost twice the adult fare, but allowed one or two adults and a combination of up to five passengers including children to travel on one ticket.

After two years of departing from inside the bus station service 74 reverted to the express stands, fighting for space amongst other services. R91 GTM (left) gives clear indication of its route about to depart from bay 15 on 15 June 1998, a few days after entering service. The second Olympian, R92 GTM (right) arrives at Drummer Street, to turn-round and take its place on the express stands a week later on 22 June 1998. **(David Slater/Trevor Brookes)**

R91 GTM at the original service 74 stop outside the old Norfolk and Norwich hospital (left), having just worked the 0630 journey from Cambridge. The destination blind is set for the return journey, which would depart from a stop on the opposite side of the road at 0905. After October 1998 permission was granted to use Surrey Street bus station in Norwich (right) from where the same bus is seen departing at a later date. **(Ken Worland/Author`s Collection)**

In an effort to avoid duplication on service 74 at peak periods, a pair of new Volvo Olympian double-deckers with Northern Counties Palatine II bodies arrived at the end of May. After driver familiarisation they entered service on 10 June. With curved windscreens they looked impressive and were heavily route branded in Blazefield style, including a map of the route above the off-side front wheel. Fitted with 68 high back dual-purpose seats and registered R91/2 GTM, the matching fleet numbers fitted into the Sovereign double-deck series. Although they were the first double-deckers in the CCS fleet, they were not the first or last to operate from Kilmaine Close. The last of the PT AEC Bridgemasters may have made a brief appearance there before the ex-London Transport DMS Fleetlines arrived in 1985. AirLinks would also base some Alexander-bodied Volvo Olympians there that were engaged on Airbus services between Stansted and London a few years later. While awaiting delivery of the Olympians, several hired coaches were used on service 74, including various coaches from Kenzie`s of Shepreth and B264 KPF, the familiar Leyland Tiger from Sovereign, now smartly repainted in the blue/cream Sovereign livery. Also hired from a dealer was a plain white Plaxton Premiere 350-bodied Volvo registered P396 MDT.

Sovereign vehicles were frequent visitors to Cambridge. A Leyland Lynx was often borrowed to operate service 38 at weekends and one is seen in company with R92 GTM (left) at Kilmaine Close in August 1998. Leyland Tiger B264 KPF was often pressed into service at Cambridge in its various guises, seen passing through Norwich (right) returning from Lowestoft on service 74 in April 1998. **(Paul Carter/Paul Hollingsbee)**

The increased running times on service 75 resulted in later scheduled arrival times at Oxford. Despite Gloucester Green being one of the designated bus stations in the country where a 30 minute break was permitted for drivers it was not always possible to park there for the required rest period. Driving to the Oxpens coach park increased the driving time and required a 45 minute legal break, resulting in late departures on return journeys. The solution was to provide a 'shunt' driver from 20 July, who travelled to Oxford on the 0700 journey, ready to drive the 1105 departure back to Cambridge. This procedure would be followed for the next five journeys until the driver of the 1700 from Cambridge returned as a passenger on the 2105 from Oxford. As the service ran every two hours, 'shunt' drivers could spend between two and three hours in Oxford and were granted access to the drivers` room at Gloucester Green bus station.

A scenic view of M306 BAV climbing the hill out of Saffron Walden, bound for London on service 38 on the afternoon of 27 May 1997. F421 DUG can be seen in a similar location on page 37.
(David Slater)

In October a new outstation was established at Ipswich Buses depot to operate the service 76, with new local drivers recruited. The arrangements with the municipal operator included refuelling and washing of coaches, only needing to return to Cambridge for servicing and repair. When short of drivers at Ipswich a Cambridge based driver would be sent to cover the duty. I did this twice using my own car for which an allowance was paid, as well as the additional hours worked.

The old established service 38 to London was withdrawn in October 1998, as it no longer fitted the core operations of the company. The route was initially taken over by Biss Bros of Bishops Stortford, who shortened the route by moving the northern terminus from Cambridge to Linton. In October 2000 Burtons Coaches filled the gap with an X38 service between London and Haverhill, although they also found it to be un-viable, despite a council subsidy. Ironically it could sometimes be operated by coaches

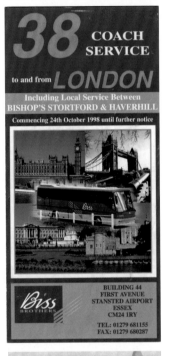

Training Officer Mac Law at the wheel of P313 CVE ready to depart from Haverhill bus station on service 38 on the last day of operation in October 1998. **(Chris Moody)**

bearing the Premier Travel Services name and driven by drivers who had previously been employed by the original Premier Travel at Haverhill. The service 74 timetable which took effect on 25 October showed that the stop in Norwich had moved from outside the Norfolk and Norwich hospital into the bus station at Surrey Street, a long-held ambition that had eluded Ian Roberts.

Drivers` wages were increased from £5.62 to £5.85 in November. The following month four new coaches arrived, like the double-deckers they were registered by Sovereign at their local vehicle licensing office with former Bedfordshire registration letters as S320/22-4 VNM, with matching fleet numbers. As the previous new CCS coach had been numbered 315, fleet numbers 316-8 had been taken by new Volvo/Plaxton Premiere 320 Sovereign coaches in Green Line 797 livery. 319 was still allocated to G519 LWU and the registration number 321 was not issued, as it was regarded as 'desirable' by the DVLA and commanded a premium, although the previous CCS coach numbered 321, F421 DUG had left the fleet a few months earlier.

The air-vent on the off-side panel identifies the long-wheelbase Volvo B10M-SEs as can be seen on S322 VNM (left) just arrived at Drummer Street in June 1999 and S324 VNM (right) at Kilmaine Close. **(David Slater/Ken Worland)**

Although the new vehicles were similar in appearance to the other Premiere 350s, they only seated 48 and had the added refinements of air conditioning, toilets and cruise control, the latter feature being a first for CCS vehicles. These coaches were part of a small number of B9M chassis to be cut by Plaxtons, who extended the wheelbase and inserted a sub-frame which allowed a capacious full-width luggage locker to be fitted behind the front wheels. This feature was most welcome by drivers, particularly on airport services where luggage for different destinations could be kept in separate lockers. This modification added £3k to the cost and reduced the rear overhang without increasing the overall body length of 12 metres, leading to a chassis designation of B10M-SE. The longer wheelbase also required more care when turning corners.

The Blazefield Group contingent lined-up at Duxford for the 1998 Showbus Rally, in between the traditional showers. Volvo Olympian R91 GTM is joined by two Wright Renown-bodied Volvo B10BLE single-deckers, R122 HNK from neighbouring Huntingdon & District and R531 TWR which had made the long journey south from Keighley & District. **(Mac Law)**

Another new service commenced on 19 December numbered 77, following on from the most recent route number 76. The previous service 77 which had only operated as a single journey (0200 Cambridge – Stansted – Gatwick direct) continued as a service 79 journey. With a 50 minute running time and ten minute turn-round, the seven return journeys

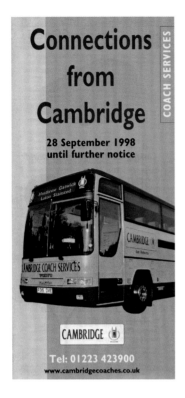
In line with the latest timetable format, a leaflet showing diagrammatic plans of routes and locations served was issued in September 1998.
(David Slater Collection)

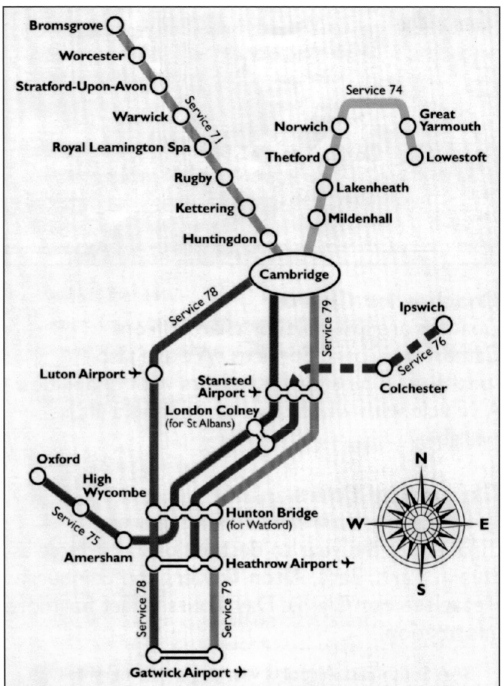

Taking a break at Stevenage Dane Street bus station before returning to Stansted Airport on the short-lived service 77 is Plaxton Premiere 350-bodied Volvo M301 BAV.
(John Law)

starting at 0520 between Stevenage and Stansted Airport could be operated by a single coach, changing drivers at Stansted. I spent an easy day learning this short route with fellow-driver Brian Camps in January 1999 but never had a chance to drive the service as it was withdrawn on 13 March 1999. A Jetlink service that passed through Stevenage on its way from Luton Airport to Stansted provided a replacement. Service 71 ran to Bromsgrove for the last time on 20 December. The outstation at the former Rover Coaches depot was closed and the remaining staff made redundant. Once again, limited service 75 and 79 journeys were operated on Boxing Day.

Chapter 5 THE BEGINNING OF THE END

The only occasion that a relief coach on service 74 had been required towards Cambridge was 27 July 1997, when Paul Hollingsbee parked his Semmence coach RJI 5723 next to P315 DVE at Kilmaine Close. **(Paul Hollingsbee)**

A familier scene to drivers arriving for duty in January 1999. G519 LWU stands ready for the next departure to Oxford on service 75, N310 VAV showing route 78 for its next journey to Gatwick via Luton and Heathrow airports, with a spare coach over the pit. The author and many others would have been happy to continue in this routine but there would be changes within a year. **(David Slater)**

Resplendent in partial fleet livery, Leyland Tiger B264 KPF displays **L** *plates that indicate its primary role at Cambridge, after serving there from time to time in several different liveries over the years.* **(Ken Worland)**

With a modern fleet of coaches driven by smartly-uniformed and well-trained drivers, Cambridge Coach Services (CCS) continued to thrive. The high profile image was well regarded by the travelling public, also catching the attention of larger organisations, particularly the successful airport network that had evolved over the years. The original policy of promotion from within that had been encouraged by Ian Roberts continued, with many drivers moving up through the ranks to be acting controllers, then if proved suitable becoming full-time controllers, entailing a change in uniform colour from blue to black. Drivers with practical skills were also encouraged to transfer to the workshop, where some of them made a valuable contribution. The 100% pass-rate for advanced driving tests was also impressive but minor collisions were still too frequent for the Blazefield Claims Director's liking. The company had a £25k excess which meant that all so called 'minor damage' had to be paid for by CCS. The high mileage and intensive nature of operation no doubt contributed to this aspect.

Elderly Leyland Tiger B264 KPF made another appearance at Cambridge in February, recently repainted in CCS grey/blue but without the diminishing blue stripes, the CCS logo was applied above the rear wheels instead of the usual position above the front wheels. Used mainly for driver training, it was sometimes used on the 0645 service 74 journey from Thetford to Cambridge. This proved convenient for Roy Edmonds, one of the training officers who lived near Wymondham and parked a coach over-night at the Semmence depot. Neighbouring Huntingdon & District, also a Blazefield company at the time borrowed it and rail replacement work for associated train company West Anglia Great Northern (WAGN) kept it busy, along with other company vehicles when needed.

Seen at Irchester Country Park in April 1999, while engaged on Private Hire is the final addition to the fleet of Cambridge Coach Services, Plaxton Premiere 350-bodied Volvo B10M, T325 APP. **(Ken Worland)**

About to depart from the coach park at the two Holy Shrines at Walsingham in Norfolk carrying some disabled passengers, who no doubt appreciated the special wheelchair lift fitted at the rear of the coach in July 1999. **(Geoff Mills)**

Driver Jim Woodburn and Marketing Manager Mary McGuire demonstrate the features of the wheelchair lift fitted to T325 APP. **(Jim Woodburn Collection)**

The opportunity was taken to display the disabled access to T325 APP at the Showbus Rally at Duxford in September 1999. **(David Slater)**

What turned out to be the last new coach delivered to CCS arrived in February 1999. This was originally intended to be S-registered but due to problems with the installation of the wheelchair lift it did not enter service until March, becoming T325 APP. The twentieth new Plaxton Premiere 350 to join the fleet, 325 was mounted on a standard Volvo B10M chassis. Although 52 reclining seats were fitted to the usual CCS specification, this coach was fitted with a rear nearside wheelchair lift to allow easy access for disabled passengers when some seats were removed. A significant amount of this type of private hire was still operated for regular clients built up over the years by Jim Woodburn with D350 KVE, the Van Hool-bodied coach with similar facilities that it replaced. The mechanism for the lift was less compact, taking up the bottom section of the entire rear luggage boot, making the new coach unsuitable for busy airport work.

Timetable changes introduced on 11 April saw the stop on service 74 in Great Yarmouth return to the Market Gates. For the 'summer peak' an additional stop was located on Marine Parade between 1 May and 26 September on through journeys to Lowestoft. This new stop was also the terminus for the last evening journey that had not previously gone beyond Norwich, giving passengers the opportunity for a long day in Great Yarmouth, returning at 2105. A tenth journey on service 75 to Oxford was introduced, leaving Cambridge at 2300, returning from Oxford at 0500. This was truly a 'night shift', so was rostered for five consecutive nights. I only drove it once, with almost three hours in Oxford and no shunt driver it was possible to keep the same coach and park in the Oxpens coach park long enough for some sleep. With 10 hours 50 minutes pay time, it was also a good earner without too much hard work. I worked out that the next time I was due on that shift that I would take a week's holiday, as I found that my sleep pattern was disrupted more than an early morning start, which I was not fond of either.

For many years Cambridge had been regarded as 'cycle-city', mainly because of the large number of students who relied on two wheels as their means of transport. Severe traffic congestion was another well-known claim to fame, exacerbated by the narrow city centre streets. Access to the coach bays adjacent to Drummer Street Bus Station was often difficult, with congestion in both directions. Cambridgeshire County Council tried various restrictions to ease the flow of traffic, the most controversial being the closing of Bridge Street and Emmanuel Road to all vehicles except buses, taxis and cycles. As previous 'buses only' and 'no right turn' signs were frequently ignored, a physical barrier was introduced in the form of rising bollards. The introduction of bollards in Emmanuel Road on 25 August 1999 only allowed authorized vehicles fitted with 'transponders' to pass. Drivers of other vehicles who still chose to ignore the numerous warning signs found their path blocked by a steel post. Those who 'tailgated' authorised vehicles often found the front of their vehicles lifted up off the ground, as the ascending bollard smashed through the sump of the engine, causing much damage and inconvenience to themselves and other traffic.

Some high profile cases challenged the County Council to remove the bollards, although they have proved their worth in reducing traffic in certain parts of Cambridge, despite causing an increase elsewhere. All CCS coaches were fitted with 'transponders' which activated the bollards, allowing them to pass through the restricted area to reach Drummer Street quicker at peak times. Traffic from Drummer Street to Parkside was also reduced, enabling departing coaches to leave the terminus with less delay. The 'transponders' also enabled coaches to use the bus lanes on Newmarket Road and Trumpington Road.

Rumours had been rife for some time that Blazefield Holdings intended to sell CCS, in line with the reduction of their operations in the south of England. Commercial Director David Hurry informed staff representatives on 20 October that the company had been sold to AirLinks, The Airport Coach Company, who were part of the National Express Group with effect from 0200 on 30 October 1999. This was confirmed in a letter to staff the following day (page 72). On 29 October CCS staff received a letter from AirLinks Managing Director John Harrison (page 73) welcoming us to his company, with the assurance that there would be 'no changes for the foreseeable future.' Having heard that term before in my career, I was aware how flexible it could be. I did not have to wait long to find out. An early indication of changes ahead came in the form of a memorandum to operating staff from Roger Birch on 11 November stating that all CCS and AirLinks tickets would become inter-available between common points. Signs indicating that National Express (NatEx) tickets would be accepted were applied to CCS coaches. Drivers from both companies were also authorised to drive all vehicles, enabling practical integration, initially to cover for breakdowns.

The entire nation seemed to be obsessed with the looming end of the twentieth century, extensive plans were made for all sorts of celebrations on New Year`s Eve to see in the new millennium. The country seemed set to grind to a halt, amidst concerns that an unprecedented 'millennium bug' might cause computers which played such a vital role in daily life to crash, unable to cope with the change of date for which they had not been programmed. This was a genuine fear that proved to be unfounded. In anticipation of the mass shut-down, when no aircraft were expected to fly for fear of the 'millennium bug' causing their complex systems to fail, the timetables published on 24 October showed many reductions in journeys over the Christmas and New Year period. I could not have imagined that Ian Roberts would have agreed to such drastic action. Some of the journeys cut short would benefit me as I was rostered on the 2000 service 79 to Gatwick on Christmas Eve, which along with the 1900 service 78 terminated at Heathrow with the subsequent cancellation of the return journeys. Driving T325 APP, the newest coach, I returned to Cambridge out of service, still claiming the full duty pay of 8 hours 25 minutes. As 27/28 December were rest days for me, I was fortunate to have four days off over Christmas.

New Year`s Eve the following Friday was even more rewarding, as I was rostered on the 1700 service 75, which was only scheduled to run as far as Stansted Airport in the wind down to the new century. As there were no passengers on board when I left Drummer Street, I crossed my fingers that none would be waiting at Addenbrooke`s Hospital. My luck was in, as I stopped in the deserted bus layby to phone the duty controller who told me to return to Kilmaine Close. New Year`s Eve had also been declared a bank holiday and AirLinks had offered £150 bonus to everyone who worked. For my two hours work I was paid the full duty pay plus the bonus, equating to £100 for each hour worked. As I wrote in my diary at the time, the last of six embossed with the CCS King`s College logo, I would never earn that much in an hour again, and I have not!

CAMBRIDGE COACH SERVICES

Cambridge Coach Services Limited
Roberts House
Kilmaine Close
Cambridge
CB4 2PH
England

Telephone (01223) 423900
Fax (01223) 423030

DJH/gmn   21st October 1999

Dear Jim

A number of rumours have been circulating recently regarding the possible sale of Cambridge Coach Services.

Yesterday Staff Representatives were advised that the business of CCS is being sold to Airlinks, The Airport Coach Company Limited to be effective from 0200 hrs on Saturday 30th October.

Cambridge Coach Services has for a number of years been a wholly owned subsidiary of Blazefield Holdings Limited. Blazefield is a private group within the Bus and Coach industry and as most of you will be aware has bus operating interests in Yorkshire, Hertfordshire, Cambridgeshire and London. Considerable investment has been put into the Cambridge Coach Services business in recent years with the expansion of it's service network; the purchase of Kilmaine Close; and modernisation and standardisation of the coach fleet.

Further growth potential would be limited under Blazefield's continued ownership, so the Blazefield Board of Directors has resolved that the future of CCS would be best placed in the hands of a larger coach operating group.

Airlinks have assured Blazefield that CCS will continue as a separate subsidiary company retaining its current identity and livery for the foreseeable future. The freehold of the premises at Kilmaine Close and the present coach fleet all pass to Airlinks ownership, and whilst their main office is in Feltham, operations at CCS will continue to be controlled from Cambridge under Roger Birch who continues as Operations Manager.

Due to the change in ownership it has been necessary to set up a new company as a legal entity into which the business of CCS will transfer. That new company currently has the title of G.A.C. No. 175 Limited and it will be re-named Cambridge Coach Services Limited at the time of transfer of the business. It is necessary therefore for the employment of all CCS staff to transfer into that company necessitating the issuing of P45's as a formality.

Terms and Conditions of all Cambridge Coach Services employees will remain unchanged with the transfer of ownership and is protected within Employment Law under 'Transfer of Undertakings Legislation'.

A new Operators Licence is also necessary requiring green discs in coaches to be changed, but all the company's operations continue as previously, or as already agreed for variations for the winter timetables.

The only person leaving the business will be myself as I will be remaining with Blazefield. However as I am the designated Transport Manager on the new Operator's Licence for the sake of continuity I will continue to be around at Kilmaine Close until the end of November, so will be able to assist with the transitional period.

Airlinks Directors will be on site at Cambridge frequently during at least the first week of their ownership and will introduce themselves to as many staff as possible.

As I have personally been involved in the development of the Airport Services since I first joined Premier Travel Services in 1982 (in those days a maximum of three journeys a day, between Cambridge and Heathrow only) I hope that I will be able to look on with envy at further developments that may occur in the future.

On behalf of the Blazefield Group may I thank everybody for their service, loyalty, and professionalism at Cambridge Coach Services and wish you the very best for the future.

Yours sincerely

David Hurry
COMMERCIAL DIRECTOR

AirLinks
THE AIRPORT COACH COMPANY LTD

683 Armadale Road
Armadale Road
Feltham
Middlesex
TW14 0LW

29 October 1999

To all employees of Cambridge Coach Services Ltd

Acquisition of Cambridge Coach Services Ltd (CCSL)

Dear New Colleague

It is my pleasure to welcome you as a future new employee to our company. You will have been made aware that the CCSL business has been acquired by AirLinks with effect from 30 October 1999.

I and members of the AirLinks team will be speaking to you collectively and individually over the next few days to explain who and what we are. Part of our task will be to reassure you that the acquisition of CCSL is a very significant and important step for us and that you, as an individual driver, clerk, fitter, supervisor or manager, are an extremely important part of the business.

Within this pack is information about the National Express Group, of which we are a subsidiary company, information about AirLinks and also included are details of how the transfer is likely to affect you and your job.

Whilst the next few days and weeks are likely to be unsettling for you, it is important for the long term security of the business that we all ensure that the delivery of services to our customers is not disrupted, and I look forward to your continued support in this.

I look forward to meeting you and to working with you in the future.

Yours sincerely

John Harrison
Managing Director

These three timetables (right) show how quickly the colours and images used changed from grey and blue to green in the interim period in the year 2000.

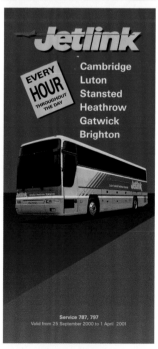

NewsLinks
AN AIRLINKS PUBLICATION

SPECIAL EDITION

CAMBRIDGE COACH SERVICES JOINS AIRLINKS

The Staff Notice, issued on 29 October 1999, gave some outline details of the agreement between Blazefield Holdings Ltd and ourselves to acquire Cambridge Coach Services Ltd (CCSL). The deal, which was completed on 29 October 1999, became effective at 0200 on 30 October 1999.

CCSL is the main operator of scheduled express services on the Cambridge to Stansted/Heathrow/Gatwick and Ipswich to Stansted/Heathrow/Gatwick corridors and it also operates a Cambridge to Oxford service. In addition it provides a bus service between Lowestoft and Cambridge as well as performing private hire and excursion work. All of these services are supported by dedicated operations, engineer-

ng and marketing teams based at Roberts House in Cambridge.

Currently there are over 100 full and part-time staff all of whom will transfer into AirLinks as from 30 October 1999. The operation is currently managed and controlled from a site in Cambridge and this site has been acquired as a part of the deal. In addition a number of vehicles and drivers are out-stationed in Ipswich and this will continue.

John Harrison, Managing Director, said "I am delighted with this acquisition and would like to welcome all of CCSL's employees to AirLinks and National Express Group's coach division. The addition of CCSL significantly strengthens AirLinks, positioning the company as the UK's leading provider of sched-

uled express services to the London airports. It will also provide more varied job opportunities for staff throughout the combined business, as well as enhanced promotion prospects"

Richard Birch, Operations Manager of CCSL added "This is a good move for CCSL as AirLinks core business is airports and a significant part of our business is linked to the movement of airline passengers. With the current and forecast expansion of Stansted airport there are great opportunities for the CCSL operation being closer to Stansted than any other part of AirLinks."

NewsLinks welcomes the CCSL team and looks forward to their future contributions.

Chapter 6 MILLENNIUM AND BEYOND

The new company diary issued to staff was embossed '2000 MILLENNIUM', with 'CAMBRIDGE COACH SERVICES' (CCS) in the familiar Friz Quadrata typeface at the bottom of the cover. The first few months of the new century were surprisingly uneventful, with CCS drivers continuing to drive CCS coaches on CCS routes wearing CCS uniforms. In February management announced plans to staff for expansion at AirLinks Cambridge depot. Extra drivers were required, resulting in the expansion of the driving school to include the training of new drivers under Mac Law, Roy Edmonds and Andy Keeble, who had also worked for CCS with previous experience in this role. Suitable training vehicles in the form of several Iveco midi-coaches were transferred from AirLinks Feltham depot but not used in service.

The route branding for service 76 mentioned below can be seen here on N310 VAV in Colchester bus station in March 2000. **(Trevor Brookes)**

The author realised in April 2000 that drastic changes were imminent, so decided to set the blind on coach 324 to show service 77 to GATWICK AIRPORT for his camera, a destination that was not usually seen in daylight. **(Author)**

Early in 2000 a form of route branding was applied to the N-reg coaches mainly engaged on service 76. The words IPSWICH, COLCHESTER, STANSTED and HEATHROW were applied in grey lettering on to the blue stripes on both sides but were not carried for long. The first visible signs of change to the coaches appeared in February, with the removal of all CCS logos and the blue blocking along each side. This distinctive feature had formed the easily identifiable part of the livery since being introduced by Premier Travel (PT) on their first batch of Leyland Tigers in 1982.

There was a period in March and April 2000 between removal of 'CAMBRIDGE COACH SERVICES' logos and application of Jetlink lettering, when many coaches appeared like this.
(David Beardmore)

Most of the coaches continued in service wearing basic grey/blue colours until new vinyls in matching blue were applied, proclaiming *'Jetlink'* in large bold lower case lettering to the same style as carried in yellow on existing Jetlink coaches, with a small 'Cambridge Coach Services' fleet name below in early April. The name of the airports served was also carried on both sides where the diminishing stripes had been. The term 'AirLinks Cambridge' was used but not widely advertised.

Staff bulletins continued under AirLinks, with General Manager Roger Birch announcing in early March that the expansion in service developments would commence on 2 April 2000. The only service not to change at that time was the service 74 to Lowestoft. The airport routes would be integrated into Jetlink services over common routes and re-numbered in the Jetlink 'Boeing Aircraft' series. Service 75 to Oxford would be re-numbered 757 and many intermediate stops would be removed to speed journey times. Combined with a new service between Cambridge and Oxford via Luton to be numbered 767, an hourly service throughout the day and most of the night would be provided. Service 76 between Ipswich, Colchester, Stansted and Heathrow would become service 737 running to the same frequency.

Leaving Luton Airport on the last leg of its journey from Brighton on service 787 in July 2000, S324 VNM has not yet had the single track route number blind replaced by one showing three numerals. **(M.A.Penn)**

Although the Jetlink name overshadowed that of Cambridge Coach Services, this close-up of coach 314 shows that the legal lettering beside the front wheel remained the same. **(David Slater)**

If coaches could talk, would M307 BAV recall taking part in the UK Coach Rally on Madeira Drive in Brighton (page 48) exactly six years earlier, just a few hundred yards away from the Jetlink terminus in Pool Valley where it is seen on 23 April 2001. **(David Beardmore)**

Due to the restricted luggage capacity and a contentious rear-end advertisement (page 83), T325 APP would usually operate the service 767 to Oxford, seen here entering Luton bus station in March 2001. **(Alan Conway)**

More drastic changes were to the 78/79 services from Cambridge to Heathrow and Gatwick via Luton or Stansted airports respectively, which unsurprisingly became services 787/797. What was surprising was that they were extended from Gatwick to Brighton and given a running time of just over 4 hours from Cambridge. Combined with other Jetlink and National Express (NatEx) services, this provided 38 journeys each way between Gatwick and Brighton, where many airport staff lived. This all looked good on paper, but did not allow for frequent delays to coaches getting in and out of Brighton at peak times. There were often special events held in the summer and large numbers of day trippers adding to the congestion. Cambridge-based drivers would be relieved at Gatwick South Terminal by a driver from Crawley depot, who spent his time driving up and down to Brighton. Some did not seem bothered if they were delayed enough to miss a trip. Cambridge drivers had no specific rest area at Gatwick, spending their break in the terminal or anywhere they could find a quiet corner.

Departures from Gatwick to Cambridge became even more unreliable, with a knock-on effect on northbound journeys from Heathrow. The introduction of service 767, combined with existing service 787 provided an hourly service between Cambridge and Luton from 0300 to 1900. As previous Jetlink services had served Bute Street bus station in Luton town centre, the new 767/787 services also called there, although the CCS service 78 had never ventured into the dark and dingy location beneath a car park which was closed in January 2008 and soon demolished.

With Ian Roberts name once again visible above the front wheel-arch, P315 DVE departs from Luton Airport on 10 April 2000 still sporting the white on black King's College Chapel logos either side of the top windscreen, features that had been removed from most coaches on the application of the Jetlink image. **(M.A.Penn)**

N312 VAV prepares to depart from Norwich bus station at 1445 on 31 July 2001 on the long service 727 to Brighton. This batch of coaches was not fitted with toilets and their use on a journey which could exceed six hours if delayed is questionable. **(David Slater)**

All Fools day on 1 April 2000 shows a selection of AirLinks vehicles parked at Kilmaine Close ready to implement the new regime the next day. The Airbus double-deckers would operate the A6 service, the white Iveco to train new drivers and a Jetlink Scania would join in the expanded operation from Cambridge. **(David Slater)**

The long Jetlink service 747 from Brighton to Norwich with various running times of between 5 hours 20 minutes and 5 hours 50 minutes, calling at Gatwick, Heathrow, Stansted, Newmarket, Thetford, Attleborough and Wymondham was renumbered service 727. An additional stop was added at Mildenhall while still operated by Crawley and Feltham drivers. Jetlink service 777 (branded 'Flightline') linking Stansted with Gatwick Airport via central London suffered serious traffic delays approaching Victoria Coach Station (VCS) from both north and south. The successful Airbus operation that ran initially between Heathrow and Central London from 1981 had suffered badly from the opening of a direct rail link branded 'Heathrow Express' which opened in 1999.

The double-deck outline on the new Airbus timetable is of a Palatine II, not one of the Airbus Royales. Neither of the former CCS Palatines were repainted in the red livery.

The Airbus operation was sold to AirLinks by London United in February 2000, giving an opportunity to split the service 777 and rebrand it as A5 between Gatwick and London) and A6/A7 between London and Stansted. This provided a half-hourly service with alternate journeys running via Stratford or Hendon. The expanded Airbus routes were to be operated by AirLinks from the West Ramp coach park at Heathrow (A2), Crawley depot (A5) and Cambridge depot (A6/A7). Airbus services were operated by a modern fleet of 19 long-wheelbase Volvo Olympians with stylish Alexander Royale bodies, fitted with wheelchair lifts in the front platforms. Providing space for a wheelchair and extensive luggage racks within the wheelbase left room for only nine seats at the rear of the lower deck. With 43 high-back seats on the top deck and air conditioning there were no opening windows. N124-30 YRW were allocated to Cambridge, supplemented by the original pair of CCS double-deckers as mentioned later.

During the second week of operation of service 767, driver Nick Hoyos pulls N311 VAV around the tight turn at the top of Luton Airport bus station on 10 April 2000 on his way to Oxford. **(M.A.Penn)**

AirLinks continued to honour existing commitments with T325 APP, the disabled access coach. Passengers have taken a break here at Birchanger Services, close to Bishop's Stortford on 2 December 2000. **(Paul Carter)**

The ending of private hire and day tours was also announced, apart from specialised hires with 325, the coach equipped with a wheelchair lift. The last CCS extended day tour ran on 1 April 2000 to Brugge, ending what had previously been an important part of operations at Cambridge, the new owners choosing to concentrate solely on airport-related routes.

The author took his camera with him to record his last journey on service 74 driving a double decker. R92 GTM is parked in the bus station at Lowestoft, in company with local Eastern Counties buses. **(Both Author)**

My experiences of the last days of CCS were driving double-decker R92 GTM to Lowestoft on the 0830 service 74 from Cambridge, returning at 1300 on 23 March. All lettering and route-branding had been removed, apart from the small fleet name below the lower rear window. The following day I reluctantly joined other drivers in the Transit minibus for a second route-learning session on the A6/A7 Airbus routes in and out of London. I was so disheartened that I took the next two days off as unpaid leave. The final week I was rostered on the 0800 Gatwick duty, followed by two compulsory rest days, then one of my favourite duties for the next three nights, 2000 service 79 to Gatwick. On the Friday I drove down in T325 APP, handing over to the 'shunt' driver before returning with an empty Jetlink coach that would be left at Gatwick South Terminal.

After taking the required 45 minute break, I climbed aboard the first of many green Jetlink coaches that I would drive. After inserting my tachograph I was soon heading north up the M23 motorway in K77 SAS, a Van Hool-bodied Scania. Being out of service I was able to turn right onto the M25 anti-clockwise, through the Dartford tunnel and back to Cambridge. As I pulled up to the diesel pump at Kilmaine Close, Tony Graves the night shift re-fueller appeared, saying "Not another one?" I replied "This is just the start, things will never be the same again". I was correct, they were not!

My last 'proper CCS shift' was Saturday 1 April. I realised that I would be driving the last official CCS departure from Cambridge to Gatwick at 2000 in coach 307, with Jetlink vinyls applied. I was tempted to paint 'JIMS LAST RUN' on the front of the coach, as I had done on my final trip with Burwell & District Daimler Fleetline 9 DER on 9 June 1979, but thought better of it. There were no passengers from Drummer Street, so I could not inform them of the significance of the journey. I did take a photo of the coach in the dark before I left but the result was not good enough to publish here. The journey was uneventful, similar to many late runs I had driven for CCS over the previous eight years. On arrival at Heathrow Central Bus Station, I was greeted by a very anxious gentleman who had left his airline tickets and passport on the coach on its previous trip up from Gatwick to Heathrow. He was so delighted to find the mislaid items still hidden between the seats that he gave me a £20 note in appreciation. That was the best tip I had with CCS, for the least effort.

Leaving Gatwick at midnight, a trouble free run bought me back to Cambridge at 0300, where I found yet more green Jetlink coaches parked at Kilmaine Close. They were ready to go out on early runs, as it was now the 2 April and Jetlink services had commenced from Cambridge depot. Paul Crocker was on duty all night in the traffic office, updating finishing and starting drivers on Jetlink procedures and variations to the Wayfarer ticket machines. My turn came at 0330, earning me half an hour's additional pay.

My third night on the 2000 departure was very different to any I had driven before. My coach was J555 SAS, another green Jetlink Scania, I set the destination to BRIGHTON, which was not much help to passengers who could be

Two Jetlink coaches at Cambridge, each with a different history. N310 VAV stands on home territory, while K77 SAS was regarded by some as an intruder! This was the first Jetlink coach to be driven by the author, brought back to Cambridge on 31 March 2000. **(David Beardmore)**

looking for a coach to go to Stansted, Heathrow or Gatwick airports. Eventually arriving at Gatwick an hour late, another driver took it through to Brighton. The new Jetlink system appeared to suffer from 'teething troubles', as I had been expecting to take the same coach back to Cambridge after my break. I finished up with M301 BAV, which I did not mind, departing at 0105, 55 minutes late. The only consolation to me was to know that I would now be paid the AirLinks 'shift allowance' of £9 for working after 0200, a bonus that would not have been considered under previous management.

M301 BAV prepares to depart for Luton and Oxford on service 767 on 11 June 2000, while the National Express Van Hool-bodied Volvos engaged on services 305 and 350 take a break and exchange through passengers on their long journeys from Liverpool to Southend and Clacton respectively. **(David Beardmore)**

The author's first trip to Oxford on service 757 under Jetlink operations was at 1500 on Sunday 9 April 2000 with M303 BAV, seen here on arrival at the Oxpens coach park. **(Author)**

Following two rest days I continued on my rostered late turns, a mixture of Gatwick and Oxford journeys, driving both green Jetlink and grey/blue former CCS coaches. On Saturday 8 April I stayed on the coach and rode through to Brighton and back with the Crawley driver, as I thought it would be more comfortable on the coach than waiting at Gatwick. On 12 April I was due to drive my first A6 journey into London, not an event I had been looking forward to. After clocking on at Kilmaine Close, I drove a company van to Stansted where I took-over R92 GTM, the same bus that I had driven to Lowestoft on service 74 for the last time only three weeks before. Still in plain grey/blue, a large red sticker with white 'Airbus' lettering had been applied to both sides at the front between decks. Departing from Stansted at 1415, returning from VCS at 1605 with a scheduled turnaround time of ten minutes, the rush hour traffic made me late for my second trip.

My 1945 departure from Stansted on route A7 was eventually completed but by the time I reached VCS my mind was made up. I thought to myself that if I wanted to drive double-decker buses in London, I should work for London Transport. Due to the late running of the previous Airbus service, there were no passengers for my scheduled 2135 A7 departure from VCS. On the spur of the moment I decided to return empty to Cambridge, following the A6 route out of London and carried on up the A1 to Baldock, where I stopped for fish and chips. By the time I returned to the depot at Cambridge I had made up my mind that I would not be driving into London again on a regular basis.

The addition of the red Airbus vinyl was the only change in appearance to R92 GTM when the author reluctantly drove it to London, here parked beside N127 YRW, one of seven Alexander Royale-bodied Airbus Volvo Olympians allocated to Kilmaine Close. **(Author)**

After careful study of the drivers' rota, I worked out that by combining rest days, bank holidays (Easter and May Day) with five days strategically chosen holiday, I could get through the next month without performing an Airbus duty. A combination of 757/67 and 787/97 duties gave me a chance to explore other opportunities which might suit me. On 5 May I drove my last service 74 journey to Lowestoft with P315 DVE, which had lost its 'Ian Roberts' memorial lettering with the removal of its CCS logos. This was replaced soon after in a slightly lower position above the front wheels. Providing a taste of what I might be missing, I was required to drive one of the red Airbus Olympian double-deckers from Stansted to Cambridge for re-fuelling one night, as I returned from Oxford as the 'shunt' driver on service 757.

Another aspect of the new operation was the employment by AirLinks of a team of plain-clothes PCV driving instructors who travelled incognito to monitor drivers' performance. From the initial ten reports on Cambridge-based drivers, three incurred the wrath of Roger Birch for not wearing name badges. More serious was the driver who was observed peeling an orange and eating it whilst driving along the M25. Any chance of leniency being shown went out of the window, (along with the orange peel, as stated in the report!)

AirLinks had introduced many work practices to Cambridge in line with their other depots at Feltham and Crawley, with the exception of wages, which they had promised to bring into line over a phased period of time. CCS had always made drivers responsible for cleaning coaches after a shift, sometimes enforced by a wage deduction for unsatisfactory performance. AirLinks' policy was to employ cleaners and shunters on night shifts and vacancies were created at Cambridge, one of which I applied for. While still employed as a driver, I tried out the new job on 6 May from 1930 – 0400 the next morning. The timescale appealed to me and was in line with my preferred driving shifts.

My main duties were washing and shunting the increased fleet in the confined space of Kilmaine Close depot, eventually spreading to neighbouring industrial premises at night with the increased vehicle allocation. By the time I commenced my first permanent nightshift, the hours had changed to 2000 – 0430, working four on/four off. A week later times moved to 12 hour four on/four off shifts from 1930 – 0730, a bit of a culture shock for me as although I preferred late shifts, I liked to be home and in bed before the sun came up!

Some of the AirLinks night-shift crew at Kilmaine Close in February 2001. (left-right) the author re-fuelling a coach, Ron Carder, with his strap-on vacuum cleaner and Tony Graves, the long-serving 'pump man'. **(Author)**

Re-fuelling and 'dropping' of coach toilets were the main occupations of the established 'pump man' Tony Graves, who had been a regular night worker with CCS since January 1995. Tony was dedicated to his job, continuing to give loyal service with just the occasional night off. Others on the alternate nightshifts became aware of just how hard Tony worked when he was on holiday or had a night off, as between them the cleaners and shunter had to cover his duties in addition to their own.

Although it had no toilet and was equipped with a manual gearbox, the oldest former CCS coach H647 UWR was still allocated on runs to Brighton. Ready to depart from bay 15 at Cambridge (left) showing the ultimate destination on 20 January 2001 and (right) parked at Kilmaine Close towards the end of the same year. **(Paul Carter/Author)**

From my new position I was able to observe the changes and there were many, without the hassle of driving coaches in service, although my shift pattern allowed me the chance to drive on one of my four days off. On 19 August I drove what had by then become the 1945 service 79 to Gatwick in S320 VNM, returning at 0010 with M305 BAV, both still grey/blue with Jetlink/CCS lettering. I did not drive another coach in service until 23 December 2000, taking an old Jetlink Volvo down to Gatwick at 1845 and bringing back H647 UWR at 2310. This was the only former CCS Plaxton Paramount 3500 coach to carry Jetlink logos while retaining the blue broken stripes, as the manual gearbox made it suitable for driver training at the time.

As each nightshift passed, I realised that I had made the right decision to give up driving on the AirLinks rota. Few of the changes were to the liking of most of the former CCS staff but the new recruits did not know any different. The Airbus operation from Cambridge seldom ran smoothly. The red Olympians may have been suitable for the short run along the M4 motorway into Central London from Heathrow but the longer slog up the M11 was too much for them at times. The garage staff at Cambridge became accustomed to the sight of them being towed into Kilmaine Close by a Lantern Recovery truck, sometimes only because they had run out of fuel! This misfortune could occur as double-deckers had off-side fuel fillers, requiring the bus to be turned around and reversed onto the diesel pump. Doing this could disrupt the queue of coaches fitted with fillers on both sides, leading to oversights at busy periods during the night.

The number of vehicles based at Kilmaine Close now exceeded the original CCS fleet substantially, many on a quick turn-round of only hours or even minutes. Coaches were sometimes parked on roads and forecourts of neighbouring businesses at night and lack of staff car parking became an issue. Arrangements were made in April 2000 with nearby Cambridge Regional College to lease their overflow car park. Located beside the A14 road the secure compound provided enough space to park cars and coaches off the road, requiring frequent shuttles for drivers to return to Kilmaine Close. Surprisingly the CCS name board remained above the workshop doors for some time, until replaced by a large AirLinks logo just before the end of the year.

S320 VNM approaches Drummer Street from Emmanuel Road having passed safely over the rising bollards, which had by then been in use for over two years to take up a journey on service 757 to Oxford on 27 April 2002. **(David Beardmore)**

One sunny morning in July 2000 towards the end of his 12 hour night-shift, the author posed R91 GTM to show how it was necessary to reverse on to the diesel pump to re-fuel the double-deckers. The Cambridge Coach Services name-board is still visible (middle) but by the time Paul Carter visited Kilmaine Close on 22 December 2000 (bottom) it had been replaced by the AirLinks sign. **(Author/Paul Carter)**

AirLinks re-introduced the previously used Jetlink number 747 for the short-lived bi-hourly service between Cambridge and Norwich. P314 CVE is seen ready to depart from Surrey Street bus station in Norwich showing the rare destination of 'CAMBRIDGE', although Stansted Airport should not have been shown. **(Author's Collection)**

Some aspects of the new timetables that had commenced on 2 April and were scheduled to run until 24 September had proved to be unworkable, resulting in revised timetables being introduced on 9 July. The 757/767 Oxford services were given more time and most of the intermediate stops reinstated, as there had been many complaints from regular travellers who relied on the route. Journey times between Cambridge and Brighton on services 787/797 were also increased to improve reliability. A new timetable had been published on 30 April for service 74 with no expiry date. The last coach ran to Great Yarmouth and Lowestoft on 8 July, with a new service 727 timetable commencing the following day from Norwich to Brighton by the usual Jetlink route.

By September 2000 a new Jetlink service 747 was running between Norwich and Cambridge every two hours throughout the day, with nine northbound and eleven southbound journeys but it did not last for long. After working 12 hour night shifts for 16 months, I decided to once again become a part-time driver in September 2001, with occasional shunting night shifts. From 24 September 2001 a new service 728 from Stansted slotted in between service 727 journeys and the service 787 from Luton and Heathrow was also extended from Cambridge to Norwich for a while. Surprisingly the pair of former CCS Olympian double-deckers, in which most of the lower deck seats had been replaced by luggage racks to match the other Olympians, once more made their way along the A11 road on occasional visits to Norwich, operating services 728/747 in their 'buzz airlines' sponsored blue/yellow Airbus livery.

Another example of random vehicle allocation shows R100 SPK, a Plaxton Premiere 350-bodied DAF SB3000 in original Jetlink livery ready to depart on the 1545 service 787 to Cambridge, with one of the S-reg former CCS Jetlink coaches waiting to take the next service 727 through to Brighton on 31 July 2001. **(David Slater)**

Recently discovered photos reveal that the former CCS 'buzz liveried' double-deckers ran in service between Stansted Airport and Norwich, seen here on familiar territory at Surrey Street bus station (left) on 24 July 2000. Luggage racks (right) had replaced most seats in the lower deck leaving just nine seats at the rear. **(Paul Hollingsbee/Ken Worland)**

Jetlink vehicle diagrams could be complicated, resulting in coaches ending up away from home depots. This situation led to Cambridge-based coach N309 VAV appearing in Northampton on 11 May 2001 while operating service 707 from Gatwick Airport, having started the day from Crawley depot. **(David Beardmore)**

The short-lived service 728 called at Mildenhall, enabling David Slater to record the variety of vehicles used during this interesting period. P313 CVE displays route 728 Stansted Airport on the front and a 'rear wrap' for a 'Barbie' video on the back. While Ian Roberts may have considered the 'rear wrap' for the 'National Horseracing Museum' at Newmarket on M305 BAV to be tolerable, particularly as the coach would have passed the said premises in Newmarket High Street, it would have been unlikely that the garish 'Barbie' and 'Bassett's Liquorice Allsorts' advertisements would have been to his taste! **(All David Slater)**

This highly contentious 'rear wrap' was applied to the back of T325 APP on behalf of 'London Luton Airport.' (left) Understandably the authorities at Stansted Airport took exception to the wording, leading to a notice in the traffic office at Cambridge warning that anyone who allocated 325 to a duty that passed through Stansted would be sacked! Oblivious to the controversy, cleaner Ron Carder wrings out his mop nearing the end of his 12 hour night-shift. **(Author)**

Contrasts in rear ends of former CCS Plaxton Premieres' parked at Cambridge in August 2000. **(Author)**

The A6/A7 Airbus service was well patronised, leading to more vehicles being required to cope with the increased number of passengers. The red livery for Airbuses originated from the traditional London Transport colour employed by London United. Several former Speedlink and Jetlink Van Hool-bodied Scanias were painted into red Airbus livery and based at Cambridge, AirLinks added colourful vinyls depicting images of Big Ben and aircraft taking off through blue clouds to promote the service. Blue vinyl wraps were applied to the three former CCS P-reg coaches late in 2002, leaving just the front ends in red. Sponsored by an airline called 'bmi', the word 'Heathlow' was plastered along the side windows in large white letters over the blue contra-vision material. Some of the M-reg former CCS Volvos had the 'Jetlink' logos replaced by 'Airbus' in a similar style on the grey/blue livery in September 2001.

Four Van Hool-bodied Scanias that had been new to the flagship Speedlink fleet, then cascaded through Railair and Jetlink liveries now sport red Airbus colours and vinyls at Cambridge depot early one morning in June 2001. **(Author)**

Wearing the hideous 'Heathlow' advertising wrap, P313 CVE arrives in Cambridge (left) on service 787 in November 2002. Similarly adorned P315 DVE, (right) rests at Stansted Airport in company with a Jetlink coach. **(Richard Haughey/Author)**

In another short-term 'Airbus' livery, M305 BAV can be seen (left) leaving Golders Green bus station bound for Stansted Airport on service A6 in May 2002. R91 GTM (right), resplendent in 'buzz airlines' livery rests between Airbus duties at Stansted Airport in March 2003 with another soon-to-disappear Flightlink liveried coach in the background. **(Paul Hollingsbee/Author)**

Smartly repainted in 'Express Shuttle' livery M305 BAV just arrived in Cambridge on service 010 from London Victoria (left). M306/5 BAV (right) parked at Kilmaine Close amongst others from the same batch ready to take-over the 010 route from Stagecoach in August 2002. **(David Beardmore/Author)**

The M-reg Volvo coaches did not carry 'Airbus' lettering for long, as a year later the powers that be decided that as NatEx now had a depot in Cambridge, the 010 Cambridge – London Express Shuttle and Friday and Sunday 1400 service 314 to Birmingham should be run 'in house'. Volvo/Plaxton coaches M301-8 BAV were fitted with toilets and repainted into Express Shuttle livery to replace the N-reg Expressliners that Stagecoach Cambus had previously used on these routes. The shuttle livery was short lived, as the eight coaches acquired the new corporate image NatEx livery within a year. For a time, any Cambridge-based NatEx coach would operate services 314 and 010 until Burtons Coaches took on the contracts with new NatEx-liveried coaches in 2004.

Stripped of 'Express Shuttle' vinyls, M303 BAV calls at Trumpington Park and Ride in May 2003 still plain white while awaiting application of the red and blue 'blobs' to form the new National Express image. **(David Beardmore)**

Showing off the new NX livery, complete with 'AIRPORT' descriptors P314 CVE (below left) is set to depart for London on a 010 journey. The rear-end (below right), of M301 BAV also loading for London on bay 12 indicates that not all Cambridge-based coaches carried the 'AIRPORT' descriptors. **(Both David Beardmore)**

Eventually service 727 became the only Jetlink route to survive serving Norwich, although First Eastern Counties with their X4 and Coach Services from Thetford did run services to Cambridge, mainly for commuters. Neither of these lasted long, as the improved rail service between Cambridge and Norwich via Ely was quicker and more frequent. The diversions previously operated via Lakenheath and Brandon were covered by various contracted operators' stage carriage services co-ordinated by Suffolk County Council but were not well patronised over a period of time, as part of other routes between Cambridge and Thetford.

Jetlink and Airbus operations continued from Cambridge depot with a colourful selection of vehicles for a while, until new management at NatEx decided to adopt a corporate image across the fleet. Launched on 3 March 2003 the new livery on a white base featured large blue and smaller red circles, linked by a curved white arrow replacing Speedlink, Jetlink, Flightlink, Railair, Airbus, Express Shuttle and Hotel Hoppa liveries. Vehicles engaged on Airport related routes also carried red 'AIRPORT' descriptors on the rear and each side, while those on shuttle routes carried blue 'SHUTTLE' descriptors in the same positions.

Departing from Heathrow Central Bus Station on 9 March 2003 (left), S320 VNM was the first coach to lose the grey/blue colours that had represented Cambridge Coach Services for so long and was regarded by many as another nail in the coffin of CCS. One year later the same coach is parked by the gate at Kilmaine Close (right), with the new National Express logos applied.
(David Beardmore/Author)

T325 APP approaches Drummer Street on 14 May 2004 to take-up a 797 journey to Brighton via Stansted, Heathrow and Gatwick airports in full National Express livery and fitted with a toilet.
(David Beardmore)

The first former CCS coach to be repainted in the white livery was S320 VNM, returning to Kilmaine Close in March 2003. The wheelchair lift was removed from T325 APP and the nearside rear-access door sealed shut, enabling a toilet to be fitted upon repaint. Removing the lift re-instated the luggage space in the boot, enabling the coach to perform normal duties. This was ironic, as although CCS had never offered wheelchair facilities to express service passengers, changes to the Disability Discrimination Act in 1995 had seen them introduced by NatEx only the previous year. Ten years later in July 2012, the latest in a long line of NatEx Managing Directors was able to announce that over 90% of NatEx coaches were fitted with wheelchair lifts. A similar situation had occurred when CCS fitted tracker devices to their coaches, which were removed by AirLinks. A few years later NatEx began an extensive campaign of fitting similar devices to their fleet, proving another instance of CCS pioneering the use of modern technology ahead of the opposition.

What appears to be a heavy-duty luggage rack mounted on the roof of P315 DVE is in fact a modern office building behind the coach outside the depot at Kilmaine Close. If the late Ian Roberts had been looking down he would have been more concerned about the missing centre number blind than the fact that his name had been removed from the coach. **(Author)**

P315 DVE lost the 'Ian Roberts' memorial markings for the second time and also gained a toilet as part of the application of the NatEx corporate image. The remaining Jetlink coaches soon lost their respective colours to plain white, until the new vinyls could be applied overnight across the network. The 'Airbus' double-deckers also received a version of the new livery, including the former CCS pair that also appeared on service A2 between Heathrow and Central London after being transferred from Start Hill to the West Ramp vehicle allocation. The new NatEx livery soon became a common sight across the country and at Kilmaine Close, where the AirLinks sign on the front of the workshop was replaced by the new NatEx logo by November, although grey/blue 'Jetlink' labelled coaches could still be seen for a while.

Former CCS coaches seen operating unfamiliar services (left) P313 CVE loads in Drummer Street on the service 314 to Birmingham in December 2003. (right) twin coach 314 departs from Victoria Coach Station on route A6 to Stansted Airport. **(Both Author`s Collection)**

Another route unfamiliar to CCS coaches was the Virgin Trains link between Watford Junction and Heathrow Airport. Previously operated by AirLinks with coaches in dedicated 'Virgin' livery, the service was numbered VT98 as seen (left) on M308 BAV at Feltham depot in April 2005. N311 VAV treads familiar tarmac on the M25 motorway (right) approaching Heathrow Airport from Watford on the same route. **(Author/David Beardmore)**

NatEx re-introduced a tenuous link between Norwich and Cambridge in the form of a late night departure from Norwich. The terminus had by then been moved to the University of East Anglia, while still serving temporary stops in the city centre while Surrey Street bus station was being drastically rebuilt. The sole journey was renumbered from 727 to 797 and diverted through Cambridge between the stops at Newmarket and Stansted Airport. This facilitated a crew change in Drummer Street, also providing an early morning departure from Cambridge to the airports.

I often drove the Norwich to Cambridge section and was confused one night after selling a return ticket from Norwich to Cambridge, wondering how the passenger would get back to Norwich, as there was no direct coach listed in the timetable then. Not wanting the hassle of annulling the ticket and giving a refund, I decided to advise him to take a coach to Stansted and change onto a service 727. Sometime later certain night time service 727 journeys were also diverted via Cambridge, which did provide a facility for return travel between the East Anglian cities during the night.

Six months after the closure of the Cambridge depot, former CCS coaches could still be seen in Cambridge. S323 VNM arrives at Trumpington on 25 August 2005 operating the short-lived 717 route which also called at Hatfield. **(Paul Carter***)*

The pair of former CCS Olympians were operating Airbus A2 service by the time Paul Carter caught R91 GTM heading out from Central London to Heathrow Airport in August 2004. **(Paul Carter)**

On Friday 4 February 2005, two days before the closure of the Cambridge depot of National Express all the coaches seen at Kilmaine Close were in corporate livery. The company name would be the fourth and final sign above the doors. **(Author)**

Early in January 2005 staff at Cambridge received a personal letter from Peter Wilkinson, the current Head of NatEx Owned Operations. His message was that due to an extensive review of activities, Cambridge depot was no longer viable and would close at midnight on Sunday 6 February. The entire operation would transfer to the former Stort Valley Coaches depot at Start Hill, close to Stansted Airport.

To be fair to NatEx, generous redundancy terms were offered, with inducements for staff who wished to transfer to Start Hill allowing a trial of a month without loss of redundancy. My last shift for NatEx at Kilmaine Close was to take a van to Stansted on 6 February, then drive coach D319 (Y319 HUA) on the 1905 service 727 up to Norwich, returning to Cambridge as service 797. After a crew-change in Drummer Street, I returned to Kilmaine Close in a minibus for the last time to cash up and clock off. Coaches were being moved to Start Hill ready for the morning run-out and Burtons staff collected two hired coaches to enable them to operate the 787 service until two more new NX liveried coaches were delivered to them that I would also drive in the coming months.

I walked out through the gates at 0200 on Monday 7 February 2005 with many memories of the times I had spent there, also of the coaches I had driven since I first drove through those gates in a Premier Travel Alexander-bodied AEC Reliance in January 1983. The premises were advertised for sale as a Bus Depot for some time but there were no takers, eventually leading to total demolition, a sad sight!

Locked gates at Kilmaine Close with a 'For Sale' sign and wreath attached to the gates on 15 May 2005. **(Paul Carter)**

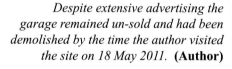

Despite extensive advertising the garage remained un-sold and had been demolished by the time the author visited the site on 18 May 2011. **(Author)**

After use on normal National Express services the last five former CCS coaches (320/2-5) received a special version of corporate livery to operate the Woking 'Railair' link. S323 VNM found its way back to Cambridge on service 787 in April 2007 (left), one month after the express coach bays had been moved from Drummer Street to Parkside. S322 VNM rests between Railair duties at Central Bus Station on 1 April 2007 (right), when the author rode on it to Woking to catch a connecting bus to the Cobham Bus Museum open day. **(Richard Haughey/Author)**

APPENDIX 1: COLLEGE CRESTS

CAMBRIDGE COLLEGE CRESTS KNOWN TO BE CARRIED BY CCS COACHES

CHRIST`S	E360 NEG	P314 CVE	
CHURCHILL	WEB 409T	YIJ 387	G95 RGG S322 VNM
CLARE	E362 NEG	M304 BAV	
CORPUS CHRISTI	F421 DUG	N312 VAV	
DOWNING	G98 RGG	S324 VNM	
EMMANUEL	G519 LWU		
FITZWILLIAM	G97 RGG		
GIRTON	F425 DUG	N310 VAV	
GONVILLE & CAIUS	E363 NEG	M302 BAV	
HOMERTON	D351 KVE		
JESUS	G96 RGG		
KING`S	G95 RGG	G62 RGG	T325 APP
LUCY CAVENDISH	H629 UWR	S323 VNM	
MAGDALENE	E365 NEG	M308 BAV	
NEWNHAM	E366 NEG	M307 BAV	
PEMBROKE	M303 BAV		
ROBINSON	F884 RFP	M306 BAV	
ST. CATHERINE`S	K392 FEG	H647 UWR	
ST. EDMUND`S	N309 VAV		
ST. JOHN`S	D350 KVE		
SELWYN	E367 NEG	E361 NEG	M305 BAV
SIDNEY SUSSEX	E358 NEG	M301 BAV	
TRINITY	F424 DUG	N311 VAV	
TRINITY HALL	P313 CVE		

*The Downing College crest (left) on G98 RGG and
Churchill College (right) on YIJ 387.*
(Both Ken Worland)

APPENDIX 2: CCS PEOPLE

My original intention was to list everyone who had worked for Cambridge Coach Services and I initially remembered about 200 names. Eventually I was able to borrow the payroll book from Roger Birch and found a total number nearer 500! This was not too surprising, as many of the names were not recalled by several of the 'old hands' that I showed the list to, although Paul Crocker remarked that "We sacked half of those!"

On closer examination of the book, some dates were shown and it became apparent that many employees did not stop long. One even started one day and left the next, many others only lasted weeks or months, long enough to collect a tie, if not the complete uniform. Although the wages were above local coach drivers rates, the intensity of the job was not always realised until after route learning with an experienced driver, the `rooky` was sent down to Drummer Street with a coach alone. Sometimes they would face an overwhelming mass of passengers, many of whom were not pre-booked and needed to be separated from ticket holders, who had priority. Not to mention the requirement to keep luggage separate for three different airports and still try to depart on time. This, along with the anti-social starting times of most shifts soon thinned them out.

I have decided to list the names that were familiar to me in line with the story coming 'from the driver's seat.' Although I worked with the Lowestoft-based drivers on service 74, I did not get to know those from the Ipswich and Bromsgrove outstations. Many of the drivers who started as full-time found other jobs, continuing as part-timers with CCS as it was often possible to 'pick and choose' their preferred shift, as I knew from experience. The rota system appeared to be the biggest obstacle to most full-time drivers.

F/P indicates full, part-time, or both, in alphabetical order below:

Allan, Trevor	F	
Alsop, Steve	F	
Appleton, Stuart	F	
Baalam, Brian	F/P	
Baker, Roger	P/F	
Barratt, Bob	F	
Bashford, Harry	P	
Bass, George	F	
Berry, Clive	P	
Birch, Roger	F	
Bird, Ron	F/P	
Botham, Mike	F	
Breeze, Gary	F	
Briggs, Martin	F	
Brown, Norman	F	
Browning, Mick	F	
Buckenham, Dave	P	
Budge, Carol	P	
Bullman, Graham	P/F	
Burridge, Paul	F/P	
Burridge, Sue	F/P	
Butcher, Chris	F	
Butcher, Shirley	F	
Butler, Chris	P	
Butters, Phil	F	
Camps, Brian	F	
Carder, Ron	F/P	
Carpenter, Martin	F	
Carr, Martin	F/P	
Carter, David	F	

Carol Budge

Brian Camps

Roger Birch

Carter, Michael	F
Cassidy, Jim	F
Cave, Steve	F
Chamberlain, Derek	P
Chambers, Dave	F
Chapman, Tony	F
Child, Grenville	F
Clarke, Dave	P
Cochrane, Geoff	F
Collins, Neil	F/P
Conquest, Charlie	F/P
Crighton, Andy	F/P
Crocker, Paul	F
Crowley, Joe	F
Darr, Jimmy	F/P
Diplock, Terry	F
Dockerill, Mike	F
Docwra, Ray	F
Edmonds, Roy	F
Edwards, Frank	P/F
Evans, Ray	F/P
Farley, Dave	F/P
Fay, Peter	F
Few, Derek	F
Forder, Clive	F
Forsythe, Hugh	P
Fuller, Brian	P
Fuller, Martin	F/P
Futter, Steve	P

Gibbs, Andy	F		Maidens, Brian	F
Gillham, Bob	F		Mallyon, Ian	F/P
Grange, Ian	F		Marshall, Derek	F
Graves, Michael	F		Martin, Tony	F
Graves, Tony	P/F		Matthews, Simon	F
Griggs, Russell	F		McGuire, Mary	F
			McLaughlan, Jim	F
Hall, Tony	F		McMordie, Steve	F
Hallam, Barry	F		McMurdo, Neil	P
Hallinan, Harry	F		Monaghan, Derek	F
Hamilton, Sid	F		Moody, Chris	F
Hauer, Robert	F/P		Moore, Grahame	F
Hayes, Stan	F		Mullen, Ben	F
Haynes, Peter	P			
Holliday, Robin	F		Nabai, Harry	F
Holt, Johnny	F		Neale, Jim	P/F
Hosier, Martin	F		Neville, Mark	F
Hoyos, Nick	P		Newbould, Jill	F
Hudson, Ian	F		Newman, Terry	F
Huffer, John	F		Nicholetti, Nick	F
Hurry, David	F		Nickson, Alan	F
Hutchinson, William	F/P		Norman, Gail	F
Hutchison, Craig	P		Norman, Roy	F
			Northrop, John	P
Impleton, Tom	F			
Inman, John	F		O`Brien, Dave	F
Innocenti, Bob	F		O`Nion, Mick	F/P
Irvine, John	P		Offord, Brian	F
Jackson, Dennis	P		Palmer, Robin	P
Jackson, Phil	F		Parsons, Mark	F
James, David	F		Patterson, John	F/P
Janes, Bob	F		Payton, Alan	P/F
Jobe, Robert	F		Pearl, Andrew	F
Johnson, Les	F/P		Peck, Nigel	F
Johnson, Rick	F/P		Pilling, Roger	F
Joseph, Chris	F		Poulter, Chris	F/P
			Prigg, Warren	F
Keeble, Andy	F/P			
Kenzie, Mark	F/P		Racher, Melvyn	F
Kidman, Alan	F/P		Raggett, Graham	F
King, Andy	F		Rankine, Alan	F
King, George	F		Ratty, John	P
Kingsman, Alan	F		Rayner, Matthew	F
Kirby, Peter	P		Read, Malcolm	F
Kirtley, Brian	F		Reay, George	F
			Rees, Richard	F
Lane, Richard	F		Rivers, Nigel	F
Law, Mac	P/F		Roberts, Ian	F
Lincoln, Steve	F		Robertson, Dave	F/P
Lockwood, David	F		Robertson, Ian	F
Lomax, Dean	F		Rudd, Kevin	F
Long, Sandra	P		Ryan, Mark	F
Lynch, Tom	F			
			Sadler, Roy	F
			Sage, Bob	P
			Sait, Kevin	F

Paul Crocker

Andy Gibbs

Bob Gillham

Scarborough, John	F
Seaber, Cliff	F
Sellars, Brian	F
Shaw, Des	F
Shaw, Martin	F
Sheppard, Mick	P
Shipp, David	F/P
Shipp, Peter	F/P
Shouls, Ian	F
Singleton, Steve	F
Slater, David	P
Smallshaw, Graham	F
Smart, Dave	F/P
Smith, Alan	F
Smith, Ashley	F
Smith, Bob	F
Smith, Colin,	F
Smith, Denise	F
Smith, Kevin	F
Smith, Martin	F
Smith, Robert	F
Smith, Wilf	F
Spooner, Kim	F
Stallard, Des	F
Stanford, Charlie	F
Stanford, John	F
Stanley, Brian	P
Stearn, Bob	P
Steele, Norman	F
Stenning, Ian	F
Stevenson, Mark	F
Stone, Terry	F
Storrie, Gary	F
Sutterby, Nigel	F
Taylor, Angela	F
Taylor, Dave	P/F
Temple, Craig	F/P
Thoday, Martin	F
Thomas, Barry	F
Thompson, Phil	F
Thornbury, Des	F
Thorogood, Anne	F
Thorogood, Mike	F
Titcombe, John	F
Toms, Peter	F
Tonks, Micky	F
Tudor, Cyril	F
Turner, Scott	F
Utting, Nigel	F

Wallace, Keith	F
Walpole, Bob	F
Walton, Tom	F
Ward, David	F
Warren, Stuart	F
Watson, Andy	F
Weaver, Barry	F
Whelan, Jim	F
Williams, Steve	F
Willis, Pete	F
Winwood, Garry	F
Wiseman, Nick	F
Woodburn, Jim	F

Simon Matthews

Harry Nabai

Brian Sellars

Chris Moody   *'The Black Tie Brigade!'*   *Mac Law*

APPENDIX 3: CAMBRIDGE COACH SERVICES FLEET LIST

Fleet No.	Reg. no.		Chassis		Body	Seats	New	In	From	Out
279	WEB 409T		AEC Reliance		Plaxton Supreme Express	C49F	1979	05/90	Premier Travel	01/93
292	VAV 254X	*R	Leyland Tiger		Plaxton Supreme Express	C53F	1982	05/90	Premier Travel	07/91
294	VAV 256X		Leyland Tiger		Plaxton Supreme Express	C53F	1982	05/90	Premier Travel	07/91
343	D343 KVE		Volvo B10M-61		Van Hool Alizee	C53F	1987	05/90	Premier Travel	10/91
344	D344 KVE		Volvo B10M-61		Van Hool Alizee	C53F	1987	05/90	Premier Travel	10/91
345	D345 KVE		Volvo B10M-61		Van Hool Alizee	C53F	1987	05/90	Premier Travel	10/91
346	D846 KVE		Volvo B10M-61		Van Hool Alizee	C49FT	1987	05/90	Premier Travel	10/91
347	D847 KVE		Volvo B10M-61		Van Hool Alizee	C49FT	1987	05/90	Premier Travel	10/91
348	D848 KVE		Volvo B10M-61		Van Hool Alizee	C49FT	1987	05/90	Premier Travel	10/91
350	D350KVE		Volvo B10M-61		Van Hool Alizee	C53DL	1987	05/90	Premier Travel	03/99
351	D351 KVE		Volvo B10M-61		Van Hool Alizee	C53F	1987	05/90	Premier Travel	03/97
360	E360 NEG	R	Volvo B10M-61		Plaxton Paramount 3200	C53F	1988	05/90	Premier Travel	12/96
361	E361 NEG	R	Volvo B10M-61		Plaxton Paramount 3200	C53F	1988	05/90	Premier Travel	12/96
362	E362 NEG	R	Volvo B10M-61		Plaxton Paramount 3200	C53F	1988	05/90	Premier Travel	02/96
363	E363 NEG	R	Volvo B10M-61		Plaxton Paramount 3200	C53F	1988	05/90	Premier Travel	01/96
364	E364 NEG		Volvo B10M-61		Plaxton Paramount 3200	C53F	1988	05/90	Premier Travel	01/91
365	E365 NEG		Volvo B10M-61		Plaxton Paramount 3200	C53F	1988	05/90	Premier Travel	11/94
366	E366 NEG		Volvo B10M-61		Plaxton Paramount 3200	C53F	1988	05/90	Premier Travel	11/94
367	E367 NEG		Volvo B10M-61		Plaxton Paramount 3200	C53F	1988	05/90	Premier Travel	11/94
#383	G95 RGG	R	Volvo B10M-60		Plaxton Paramount 3500	C49FT +	1990	10/91	Parks, Hamilton	08/98
#384	G96 RGG		Volvo B10M-60		Plaxton Paramount 3500	C49FT +	1990	10/91	Parks, Hamilton	12/98
#385	G97 RGG		Volvo B10M-60		Plaxton Paramount 3500	C49FT +	1990	10/91	Parks, Hamilton	12/98
#386	G98 RGG		Volvo B10M-60		Plaxton Paramount 3500	C49FT +	1990	10/91	Parks, Hamilton	12/98
387	FUA 393Y	*R	Volvo B10M-61		Plaxton Paramount 3200	C53F	1983	01/92	Rover, Bromsgrove	01/95
#388	F884 RFP		Volvo B10M-61		Plaxton Paramount 3500	C49FT	1989	01/92	Bleanch, Hetton-le-Hole	09/94
#389	F424 DUG		Volvo B10M-60		Plaxton Paramount 3200	C50F	1989	03/92	Wallace Arnold, Leeds	08/98
#390	F425 DUG		Volvo B10M-60		Plaxton Paramount 3200	C50F	1989	03/92	Wallace Arnold, Leeds	02/96
#392	K392 FEG		Toyota HDB30R		Caetano Optimo	C18F	1993	03/93	New	05/95
#391	F421 DUG		Volvo B10M-61		Plaxton Paramount 3200	C50F	1989	04/93	Wallace Arnold, Leeds	08/98
329	H629 UWR		Volvo B10M-60		Plaxton Paramount 3500	C50F	1991	12/93	Wallace Arnold, Leeds	10/98
319	G519 LWU		Volvo B10M-60		Plaxton Paramount 3500	C50F	1990	01/94	Wallace Arnold, Leeds	10/99
358	E358 NEG		Volvo B10M-61		Plaxton Paramount 3200	C53F	1988	01/94	Sovereign, Stevenage	12/96
359	E359 NEG	R	Volvo B10M-61		Plaxton Paramount 3200	C53F	1988	01/94	Sovereign, Stevenage	01/96

Fleet No.	Registration	Chassis	Body	Seating	Year	Date in	Source	Date out
301	M301 BAV	Volvo B10M-62	Plaxton Premiere 350	C52F	1994	10/94	New	10/99
302	M302 BAV	Volvo B10M-62	Plaxton Premiere 350	C52F	1994	10/94	New	10/99
303	M303 BAV	Volvo B10M-62	Plaxton Premiere 350	C52F	1994	11/94	New	10/99
304	M304 BAV	Volvo B10M-62	Plaxton Premiere 350	C52F	1994	11/94	New	10/99
305	M305 BAV	Volvo B10M-62	Plaxton Premiere 350	C52F	1994	11/94	New	10/99
306	M306 BAV	Volvo B10M-62	Plaxton Premiere 350	C52F	1994	11/94	New	10/99
307	M307 BAV	Volvo B10M-62	Plaxton Premiere 350	C52F	1994	12/94	New	10/99
308	M308 BAV	Volvo B10M-62	Plaxton Premiere 350	C52F	1994	12/94	New	10/99
347	H647 UWR	Volvo B10M-60	Plaxton Paramount 3500	C53F	1991	11/94	Wallace Arnold, Leeds	10/99
362	G62 RGG	Volvo B10M-60	Plaxton Paramount 3500	C49FT +	1990	05/95	Ingfield Northern Rose	12/98
#392	B490 UNB *R	Volvo B10M-61	Van Hool Alizee	C53F	1985	05/95	Rover, Bromsgrove	01/96
#349	F885 RFP *R	Volvo B10M-61	Plaxton Paramount 3500	C49FT	1989	05/95	Rover, Bromsgrove	12/96
354	B592 XNO *R	Volvo B10M-61	Berkhof Esprite 340	C49FT	1984	05/95	Rover, Bromsgrove	01/96
309	N309 VAV	Volvo B10M-62	Plaxton Premiere 350	C52F	1996	02/96	New	10/99
310	N310 VAV	Volvo B10M-62	Plaxton Premiere 350	C52F	1996	02/96	New	10/99
311	N311 VAV	Volvo B10M/62	Plaxton Premiere 350	C52F	1996	02/96	New	10/99
312	N312 VAV	Volvo B10M-62	Plaxton Premiere 350	C52F	1996	02/96	New	10/98
313	P313 CVE	Volvo B10M-62	Plaxton Premiere 350	C49FT	1996	12/96	New	10/99
314	P314 CVE	Volvo B10M-62	Plaxton Premiere 350	C49FT	1996	12/96	New	10/99
315	P315 DVE	Volvo B10M-62	Plaxton Premiere 350	C52F	1997	03/97	New	10/99
91	R91 GTM	Volvo Olympian	Northern Counties Palatine II	DP39/29F	1998	06/98	New	10/99
92	R92 GTM	Volvo Olympian	Northern Counties Palatine II	DP39/29F	1998	06/98	New	10/99
320	S320 VNM	Volvo B10M-SE	Plaxton Premiere 350	C48FT	1998	12/98	New	10/99
322	S322 VNM	Volvo B10M-SE	Plaxton Premiere 350	C48FT	1998	12/98	New	10/99
323	S323 VNM	Volvo B10M-SE	Plaxton Premiere 350	C48FT	1998	12/98	New	10/99
324	S324 VNM	Volvo B10M-SE	Plaxton Premiere 350	C48FT	1998	01/99	New	10/99
325	T325 APP	Volvo B10M-62	Plaxton Premiere 350	C52DL	1999	03/99	New	10/99

*   Indicates original registration. Subsequent registrations given in photo captions.

+   Indicates demountable toilet fitted, replaced by 4 extra seats at times, making C53F

\#   Indicates original fleet number, later renumbered

R   Indicates coach also carried ROVER name

Dates in and out of service are those known. Transfers between other group members recorded in captions to photos, where known.

APPENDIX 4: TAILPIECE

As I approach the final page I realise that my task is almost complete, looking back I wonder if I had realised what was involved in producing this book I should have continued? While many former employees have gone out of their way to help and encourage me, some people could have been more helpful. I realise that anyone working full-time found it difficult to respond and concede that I could not have achieved this project if I had been in full-time employment myself. Despite widespread appeals for information, many emails and phone calls went un-answered.

My research unearthed a tremendous amount of information I was not previously aware of. Some of the coaches featured are still on the road, engaged on less arduous duties throughout the length and breadth of the British Isles with subsequent owners, some as school buses with increased seating capacity. A few former staff survive in the employment of National Express, the successor to Cambridge Coach Services, while others take life easier with private companies and like myself only drive part-time. Many are now enjoying retirement but inevitably some have sadly passed away.

Over the years I have written to leading die-cast producers Exclusive First Editions and Corgi, suggesting they produce models in CCS livery to no avail. Corgi did produce an OOC model of T325 APP in National Express 'AIRPORT' livery and I have repainted several Corgi models in the iconic colours myself. (see below).

Various items of memorabilia (above right) carrying the company logo and subsequent designs of staff name badges (below).

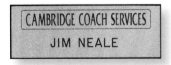

Contrast in coach rear-ends, (above) is a selection comprising Plaxton Supreme, Paramount 3200 and 3500 models with a lone example of a Van Hool Alizee photographed by David Slater at 0700 on 18 August 1992. By the end of 1994 the scene was very different, with (below) the eight new Plaxton Premiere-bodied Volvo coaches lined-up on Christmas Day just as they had returned from service the previous night in various states of cleanliness. **(David Slater/Chris Moody)**

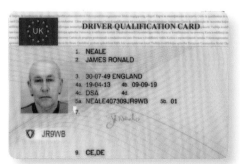

When I wrote the introduction on pages 4/5 many months ago, I indicated that my coach driving career could be cut short. Since then I have completed 35 hours of compulsory training, resulting in the awarding of a Certificate of Professional Competence and the Driver Qualification Card seen (right). This card is valid until 09-09-2019 and subject to me passing annual medical examinations would allow me to occupy 'the driver`s seat' until just beyond my seventieth birthday! It is also the twenty first century equivalent of my PSV driver`s badge (left) for which I paid 5 shillings (25 pence) deposit in 1970.

Back Cover: An image of what might have been... created by Vaughan Allanson.

£15

Cambridge Coach Services
from the Driver's Seat
by Jim Neale

ISBN 978-0-9575996-0-4

Published by Burbus Publications

9 780957 599604 >